EARTHY
MYSTICISM

More Praise for *Earthy Mysticism*:

"Through tears and laughter, Tex Sample moves us from remote piety to the clear awareness of God-with-us in the midst of all of life. These stories from a master storyteller give words to the "un-talk-about-able" nature of God, leaving one breathless with awe."

—**Jane Allen Middleton**, Resident Bishop Harrisburg Area, The United Methodist Church

"It ought to be official: Tex Sample is a 'national treasure.' From one of the world's greatest living storytellers, this book showcases a master at work, one who knows the value of lifting up stories he stops just short of telling."

—**Leonard Sweet**, Drew Theological School, George Fox University, www.sermons.com

"Tex Sample weaves together heaven and earth, grit and glory, unveiling a God who is shockingly present. This is spirituality shaped by the streets; mysticism embodied by a motorcycle gang; raucous resistance to a narrowing religiosity that confines spirit to sanctuaries and salvation to the churched. In these holy, haunting, healing stories, Tex unleashes a disruptive invitation to dance with the God of surprises into the fullness of life."

—**Janet Wolf**, pastor, preacher, professor, and community organizer

EARTHY MYSTICISM

SPIRITUALITY FOR
UNSPIRITUAL PEOPLE

TEX SAMPLE

Abingdon Press, *Nashville*

EARTHY MYSTICISM
SPIRITUALITY FOR UNSPIRITUAL PEOPLE

This book is printed on acid-free paper.

Library of Congress Cataloging-in-Publication Data

Sample, Tex.
   Earthy mysticism : spirituality for unspiritual people / Tex Sample.
      p. cm.
   ISBN 978-0-687-64989-1 (binding: pbk., adhesive, perfect : alk. paper)
   1. Spiritual life. 2. Sample, Tex. I. Title.
   BV4501 . 3 .S253 2008
   248.4—dc22

                                                           2007051096

All Scripture quotations are from the New Revised Standard Version of the Bible, copyright
1989, Division of Christian Education of the National Council of the Churches of Christ in the
United States of America. Used by permission. All rights reserved.

Some material from chapter 6 was previously published in Tex Sample, *Powerful Persuasion:
Multimedia Witness in Christian Worship* (Nashville: Abingdon Press, 2005).

Every effort has been made by the author to secure permission from those who are identified by
name and quoted directly or described indirectly in this book. Names and specific identifying
information for other persons have been modified at the discretion of the author to protect
privacy.

08 09 10 11 12 13 14 15 16 17—10 9 8 7 6 5 4 3 2 1
MANUFACTURED IN THE UNITED STATES OF AMERICA

ACKNOWLEDGMENTS

I am indebted to a good many of my friends who read part or all of what is here. This book would be much better if I could do all they suggested, but it would be much worse without what I could do after they named it. So, heartfelt thanks to Kenneth Carder, Al and Donna Denman, Gilbert and Dorris Ferrell, Gene and Sarah Lowry, Gene and Karen Sue Spencer-Barnes, Bascom "Dit" Talley, Bill Hickok, Gloria Vando, Robert Day Sartin, Bert Montgomery, Laurie Beth Jones, Shelly Buckner, and Bonnie K. and Bruce Williams.

Always there is Peggy Sample. She listened to me read these stories out loud too many times. She is fresh air and warm sunshine on any dark day, and always reason enough to celebrate life together.

Dedicated to the people of the Asbury United Methodist

Church in Phoenix, Arizona.

This diverse community of faith

is the ongoing site of an earthy mysticism.

CONTENTS

A GOD WHO WILL GOOSE YOU

alking across an area called the Quadrangle at Louisiana State University late one night, I remember a slight rustle in a tall oak above me. A soft breeze, one current of a stray flow of air, touched these few small limbs at the top of this huge tree. I then chilled, not the chill of being cold, but of being in the presence of Something Enormously Vast. At first it seemed Strange but not alien. It seemed Otherworldly and yet encompassed this world. I felt a kind of fear not so much of a threat but of an exposure to a Reality I had never known.

I kept walking trying not so much to escape this Moment but to test it. My first thought was that I was just scared, afraid of walking at night by myself. But I then remember being caught up in an Infinite Void. I continued to experience myself as walking, but my own body and the earth beneath my feet, the Quadrangle, and everything about me seemed to participate in this Inexhaustible Space, this Abyss of Reach without limit.

I suddenly felt Embraced, as though this Reality, inexhaustible in its height and depth and breadth, had incorporated me as a participant in a Boundless Void of Relatedness. The Emptiness took on a Connectedness, but more than that, it felt like an Infinite Caress of Love and Care. But that does not quite say it either, as though it could be said. A *caress* sounds something like an external encompass, but here the external and the internal seemed to disappear. The sense of one's deepest insides are not just searched and known but reached and touched and made one with earth and sky.

In moments like these some speak of experiencing great joy. While that was not absent, it's not what I remember most. Further, it was so much more a sense of union, but union is too abstract. It's a oneness that is molecular in its embrace, but that's too "scientific" and doesn't convey the intimate sense of being permeated with a love that does not transgress or violate. Rather it takes on the character of being ultimately Home where you were always meant to be.

This was the most powerful mystical experience I ever had, but it turned out to be the least important. I was a first-year student at Louisiana State University. I had gone there to play baseball, hoping to make the Tiger team and then be discovered by a New York scout and pitch in Yankee Stadium. I never had that kind of athletic ability, and I was running from some strange urgency that insisted that I go into "the ministry."

I absolutely hated the idea of doing such a thing. The very thought that I would have to go through life as some sanctimonious mouther of platitudes drove me crazy. That I would have to tell people things they already knew and fill their ears with a bunch of musts, oughts, and shoulds was about as exciting as standing on a corner telling people they ought to look both ways before crossing the street. I later learned, however, that the call to go into the ministry is a lot like throwing up. You can put it off for a while, but there comes a time when you have to do it.

While at LSU I majored in physical education, a series of classes in health and zoology and courses in tumbling and swimming that bored me beyond belief. To make matters worse I seriously injured my arm during the opening weeks of baseball and had to quit the team. I was worn slick with school and had no motivation for any of my classes. Academic study was like pushing a truck with a rope. I had, moreover, gone through a six-month attempt at "atheism" that year, and that didn't work either. I never really believed I didn't believe, so even my atheism failed. It certainly did not shut down the "urgency" I felt about the ministry and the sense that God was crowding my ass. Please understand, I am not blaming LSU. It was and is a fine school. I was just engaged in the wrong pursuit.

But in that mystical moment, I remember how small and petty my life appeared before me: the people I did not like, my own egoistic strivings, the silliness of my worries, and the sense that I had given myself to too little. All these things took on a stark unreality. At the same time, this was not a world-denying event. I decidedly remember the sense of gravity pressing in on me about how beautiful the world is, and how important it is to live and be a part of the world and this wild adventure of living.

I don't remember exactly how long this mystical experience lasted. It went on at least as long as it took me to walk across the Quadrangle and beyond. But the experience had a "timeless" quality about it. When I got to the stadium where my dorm was, the moment had ended.

I later learned that what I had was a form of a classic mystical experience. Such events are reported again and again in the literature on mysticism, but I had no acquaintance with such things. In my world of that time I knew about "being born again" or going to revivals and seeing people have these life-altering conversions. I understood that some of these conversions were real and some were simply attention-getting fakery. In fact, some older teenager boys and young men figured out that young women in the immediate aftermath of these "born again" experiences were particularly vulnerable to sexual seduction. These young males therefore followed the revivals looking for prey. Knowing such things and never having had a "born again" experience, I was suspicious.

Nevertheless, this mystical event would be the most important "spiritual experience" in my life up to that point. It gave me the momentum to take that step toward ministry. It gave me a sense that I could pursue the "urgency" that till then I endured as a persistent, negative, nagging, nuisance. I cannot say it changed my life. It was more a confirmation of the direction toward which I was being pushed. I would like to say that from that moment on

I was a radically different person, that this dramatic moment changed everything about me. But that's not true either. It had an impact, to be sure, but it was more of a "yes" to the cause of the turbulence in my life, that unrelenting urgency and pressure I felt.

I don't want to be misunderstood. I am grateful for that ecstatic moment I had at LSU, and it was important at that time of my life. I certainly do not wish it had never happened. But it is far from the most important mystical experiences of my life. As the years wore on, I came to find God operative in times and places quite differently. It is what I now call earthy mysticism. I say "earthy" and not "earthly." I know that *earthy* can mean terrestrial, of or pertaining to the earth, being of this world. It can mean *earthly*, and this is important in what I want to say; but this does not adequately convey what I mean. *Earthy* also means coarse or gross. It means not refined. It means simple and natural, hearty and unashamed. It means the humor that is not discrete. It involves the common and the "unclean," the profane and the seamy. It speaks in four-letter words. Further, it deals with sex and genitals, with blood and gore, and dirt and the gritty. It is the unkempt end of life and the people who so stringently represent such things. In this book you will find language that reflects this earthiness.

The problem, however, with trying to explicate earthy mysticism with a word study is that we deal here with something that cannot be defined. It certainly cannot be explained. It can only be shown. It is best shown in stories, in stories where God shows up in unexpected places, in unseemly events, and in the "wrong people." In circumstances like these I find myself in mystical states quite different from the one I had at LSU. I say quite different not in the sense that it is a different God. Rather it is that God appears in the ordinary, the common, and the coarse.

Such things trigger or evoke a different kind of mystical state, not one in which one is lifted into an ecstatic, eternal-like moment but rather some sense of an incongruent Presence of God. I have known this Presence in moments when I have participated in evil. I have known it while subjected to a barrage of obscenities or when the Redemptive Current in a situation comes from the most unregenerate source, or in the sweaty, embodied congress of sexual love. All these and more can be epiphanies of this nitty-gritty God.

What follows here is a testimony of narratives where this strange God appears. Such Appearances supply the mystical states that have come to shape my life. I am not helped much by conventional approaches to spirituality. I find it almost impossible to do "devotions." Daily Bible study in the sense of devoting twenty to thirty minutes a day never worked for me. I cannot get around to scheduled times for prayer on my knees with head bowed. I find labyrinths and prayer beads boring. I am ever and again distracted in silent meditation. I simply cannot sustain a spirituality based in such things. Yet, Bible study, prayer, worship, and Eucharist form the heart of my practices, but it is a different spirituality.

I do not regard myself as unusual or special. My hunch, and it is more than that, is that a host of people will recognize themselves in what I describe here. What is here is, clearly, my story; but it is not about me. It is about a God of surprises, of One who comes in the ordinary and the seamy. It is about a God who will goose you. It is about mystical moments when clearly the only thing that finally matters is this God who will never leave us alone, especially in the ordinary and angular places of life. It is, I hope, a spirituality for unspiritual people.

1

THE DEATH OF A BLUE JAY

"Daddy, look at those blue jays.
They are so beautiful!"
"Yeah, they are, Son, but they sure are
destructive and raise a lot of hell."

$\big\{$ teve was an absolutely adorable child. He won the most beautiful baby award at the Boston University School of Theology Baby Show, where I was in school, and made an appearance, picture and all, in the *Boston Herald* newspaper. He exuded charisma, and people loved him. He was so vitally alive.

When he was four or five years old, he ran away from home. After a frantic search his mother found him swinging on a fence down at the local grammar school. He kept saying to her, "I want to go to scool; I want to go to scool." It was not a portent of things to come. As bright as Steve was, and he was very bright, he never did well in school. From the beginning he had difficulty with reading, writing, and math. We later came to believe that he had a serious learning disability.

Within a few years he developed a deep hatred of school and everything connected with it. School became a place where he acted out, defied his teachers, and showed off for any of the kids who would pay attention, and no few did. We tried everything we knew to do: counseling, special school, and special classes. We tried gentle love at first and then tough love, but nothing seemed to work. By the time he was fourteen, he was in wholesale revolt against school, cutting class and being disrespectful to his teachers. That same year he and a friend took our car while we were away one evening and rolled it twice at eighty-five miles an hour. Both of them walked away from the wreck without damage to themselves except for a gash on his friend's cheek. This was the first of nine accidents he would have over the remaining fifteen years of his life. He walked away from everyone of them but the last one.

He had, of course, been drinking the night of the first accident, and we became aware slowly that he was also doing other drugs. By the time he was sixteen, he was an active alcoholic. He sneaked out at night and sometimes disappeared for a day or two at a time. By the time he was seventeen, he had moved out of our home. He tried the Marines, but the rupture of a large blood vessel in his leg ended his tenure there after just six weeks of boot camp. His life through his late teens and twenties was one of drug and alcohol abuse. He was in and out of jail on a regular basis. Once while he and his brother, Shawn, were being pursued by a gang, he fired a gun at the ground to slow them down, he said. The bullet ricocheted and hit one of the pursuing teens in his arm, a flesh wound that was not serious; but, when Steve violated his suspended sentence, he spent six months in the state prison in Missouri. That proved to be his last time in jail but not the end of his drug abuse.

He loved motorcycles and apparently was an awfully good rider. He drove a Kawasaki and loved beating the guys on the Harleys. He won the races that demonstrated speed, but he also won the events to determine who could ride the slowest. The latter was done by driving with a woman on the back of the bike whose job it was to take a bite from a peeled banana hanging on a string while the bike went slowly enough for such a feat to be performed. The story is also told that Steve was once being chased by police on the interstate. To escape, Steve took the bike off the road, went down an embankment, up the other side, through a field, and then onto a gravel road a mile away.

Women loved him. This made tough love difficult, because there was always a girl waiting for the chance to "help" him. He went through dozens of relationships and one marriage, but nothing seemed to help his skid into a night without stars.

During those awful fifteen years we remember long nights of lying awake wondering where he was. There were the phone calls in the early morning hours reporting an arrest or another accident. Or there were even more disconcerting calls from strange people looking for Steve that frightened us. I began to hate the middle of the night. Someone once said that there is no courage like courage at three o'clock in the morning. I remember much more cowardice than courage through those dark and difficult years. We despaired of his life changing. We spent sleepless nights and agonizing hours over his fate and his seeming inability to change.

Through those years we saw him in many painful and devastating conditions, injured after car wrecks, motorcycle accidents, and even one severe electroshock that very nearly killed him; we visited him in jails, in hospitals, in drug rehab programs, in a seemingly endless series of cheap apartments; we watched him lose one job after another, break up with at least a dozen women, and dissolve one marriage; we winced at broken noses, lacerations, bruises, and black eyes from fights; we witnessed his "decision" to go on the wagon time and again; and we spent those treadmill nights unable to sleep and gutted by worry and fear. It seemed that nothing worked and nothing seemed to be going on in his life that could pull him out of his drug dependency. I felt he was God forsaken.

When he was twenty-eight years old, he met Nancy, and they were soon engaged. Both were drug users, but that summer Nancy went into a drug rehab program, dried out, and began that long quest for sobriety. At first Steve said that was the end of their relationship, that they could never have a life together with her in a rehab program; but Nancy encouraged Steve to come into the program with her. After a couple of weeks, he did. He went cold turkey, endured the DTs and the terrible withdrawal from fifteen years of drug and alcohol abuse. Miraculously he dried out.

In a conversation with the head of the rehab center, she told him he had to get a new playpen and a new set of playmates. Steve asked where someone like him with his love of motorcycles would find such people. She told him of the Visions Motorcycle Club. This was an AA motorcycle gang that combined their love of bike riding with the struggle to stay dry and work for sobriety. From that point on he never used alcohol or other drugs again, except for copious amounts of caffeine from those endless cups of coffee he drank. These nine months became the best time of his life.

He, Shawn, and I built a solar room on our house. He won a trophy in the Kansas City Motorcycle Show and proudly showed us around to observe what had been done to the different bikes. That Thanksgiving he and Nancy went with us to see his grandparents in Mississippi. Sober, he celebrated Christmas with the family and bought presents for everyone, especially things that "aren't practical" but that "everyone will enjoy." His own hard-living life gave him a special perspective on AA, and he began speaking around the city and working especially with those who had just come out of prison. Through Visions he found a special group of friends and a vital new purpose in his life. Our friend, Sarah Lowry, offered him a new job in a chemical plant that paid enough for him and Nancy to plan to get married that summer. For the first time since he had begun drinking, he talked about his own spirituality in the sense of a Supreme Power at work in his life.

He changed. He became the person we had hoped to see for all those fifteen years. While it was evident that he struggled to take it "one day at a time," the Visions Motorcycle Club became his church and they played and prayed together. It was an amazing group of people. It was, of course, filled with those who had done no little hard living, like Steve; and yet they were all so different except in their desire to stop drinking, to live a life of sobriety, and in their love of bike riding. We found them not only ministering to Steve but to us. This motley crew of about thirty or forty men and women became his extended family and included us. I can remember phone calls from members of the group just checking in to say how well Steve was doing and that they were all working together. They would ask us to pray for them.

I remember this sense of a strange people of God drawn from walks of life very alien to respectable churches I knew. There was this very material mystical feel of a people on the move, finding their way, always trying to make it one more day. They seemed like a mobile church, searching for things to do, reaching out to each other and to others; and, of course, at times there was an almost frenetic activity to keep occupied, to be busy, to stay away from the temptations of drink and drugs. I remember a gratitude I had for them, that this motley crew was such an embodied gift of God, that their celebrations and struggles were incarnate expressions of God's activity. I often wondered how Steve could have made it and what he could possibly have done to stay sober without the Gift of this amazing group of bikers.

On the day he was killed, Steve and Nancy and another Visions couple took off for a ride in those beautiful rolling hills of rural Missouri north of Kansas City. It was an uncharacteristically warm day in February with a sun that filled earth and sky with sixty degrees of temperature and bright, golden illumination. They stopped in Smithville, and Nancy told us later that Steve ate an entire chicken for lunch and drank copious glasses of iced tea. Back on the bike they continued up Highway 169 and took a right on Route 116. This latter highway is a gently bending road up and down over undulating hills through woods and farmland. Even in a car you are mesmerized by the movement and flow of the road. It becomes itself like a chant, an occasion to thank God that highways like this exist and that the blending of machine and self and nature and world can dance in a celebration of the senses.

Nancy and Steve were on his award-winning bike from the motorcycle show two weeks earlier. There was too much paint on an electric circuit, which interrupted the work of the generator and depleted the battery. When the battery gave out, they found themselves right in front of a body shop not far from Lathrop, Missouri. As they went in to ask for help, Steve discovered the owner was a deputy sheriff. Although sober, Steve was still apprehensive about the law, so he asked the other couple to talk with the shop owner. When they approached the man, however, he could not have been more courteous or helpful. They scraped the connection and recharged the battery. The owner told them of his own son's love of motorcycles and how much the two of them loved to work on bikes. He mentioned that his son had been injured in a military-service-related accident and that he was waiting to get a flight to go see him.

Nancy, who was not seriously hurt in the accident, told us later that Steve was touched by the man's help and his sharing with them. As they were about to leave the shop, she said, Steve stopped and looked at the man standing some distance away.

"You see," she said, "Steve had been having some experiences that he simply could no longer deny. He felt that a Supreme Being was working in his life. He couldn't believe how so many things were working out for him. He just knew there was something beyond him, a power helping him straighten out his life. He just wanted things right and to do things right. And it was working."

After the other couple got on their bike and Nancy climbed on the back of theirs, she said that Steve looked at them, looked back at the deputy sheriff, and said, "You know, this shit really works."

Those were the last words anyone ever heard him say. He put on his helmet and drove six miles to the intersection of Highways 116 and 33.

As they approached the intersection, a truck was waiting at the stop sign to their left. What Nancy and Steve did not realize was that the sun, now late in the afternoon, was directly behind them. The driver in the truck simply could not see them. He had stopped twice, and when he finally entered the intersection, he collided with Steve's bike. From the look of the wreckage, it appears that Steve turned the cycle to protect Nancy. It worked.

While initially knocked unconscious, Nancy suffered an abrasion on her calf and a broken little finger; but in the collision Steve was swept under the truck, and the momentum carried them across the roadway.

A friend and former student of mine was chaplain to the police in Lathrop. One of the first people on the scene, he gripped Steve's hand and said, "If you can feel this, squeeze my hand." He felt a slight clutch. It was the only response from Steve from that moment on. In all likelihood Steve was brain dead within minutes after the wreck, but his strong constitution and great heart fought another twelve hours with his pulse at 160 beats a minute working desperately to sustain his dropping blood pressure. Finally, when his heart slowed to half that rate, the loss of blood pressure brought an end to his unconscious but valiant effort.

The wake and the funeral were held at the chapel at Saint Paul School of Theology where I taught. We were immediately surrounded by support from the school and from the Platte Woods United Methodist Church we attended. Being part of a highly devoted seminary and an extraordinarily sensitive church and its pastor was a true source of strength and comfort. What I was not prepared for was the outpouring of love and care from the Visions Motorcycle Club. There were, of course, phone calls and visits, but the impact of this came first at the wake. Not only did they show up, but they stayed and asked—almost as if they thought they would be turned down—if they could have a part in the funeral service of worship. They especially wanted to lead the

Lord's Prayer and wanted the first three rows of the chapel across from the family reserved for the Visions group. We, of course, were touched and pleased.

During the wake Peggy and I greeted people as they came in through the front door of the chapel. Steve's brother, Shawn, stood like a sentinel down by the open casket and greeted those who came to view the body. Steve's sister and our daughter, Jennifer, talked with people in the congregation. We did not know what a terrible time this was for Jennifer. One week after Steve's death, her husband left, and she found herself with two children less than four years of age. I have so often wondered how she handled her brother's death and the loss of her husband in such a very short time. It is testimony to her strength and courage that she made it through.

I remember that at one point a Reverend Bill (not his real name) came. He was a biker preacher though not a member of Visions. He approached the funeral director and stated: "I'm Reverend Bill, and I have come to see Steve." He was a massive man, weighing at least 300 pounds, and while overweight was also just big! He wore blue jeans, biker boots, and a leather vest with no shirt. His chest was hairier than my head, and the size and expanse of his furry trunk made it difficult to look at anything else about the man. The funeral director came over to me and stated with some hesitation: "This man says he's a Reverend, and he wants to see Steve."

"Well, from the looks of him, I would let him do anything he wants!" was my compliant reply.

There was such an array of people there. Theologians, clergy, staff and administrators of the seminary, people from a variety of churches in the city and its environs, bikers, friends of Steve still strung out on drugs and/or fighting the ravages of alcoholism, family, and a wide circle of other friends. They were affluent and poor, black, brown, white and gold, Ph.D.s and high school dropouts, the religious and the secular, the reputable and the disreputable. The parking lot and the streets around the school looked as if used car and motorcycle lots from every part of town had suddenly come together.

I remember the sustained and pervading sense of support that came from this strange collection of people. A sense of an unbounded Connectedness crossed the chasms of the loss. I thought to myself that with ties like these death had no capacity finally to separate us. The chapel filled with a Reality in which we participated, a Reality made clearer by the strange constellation of people there. I knew that outside that chapel we lived among walls, barriers of difference and otherness; but in the chapel for that moment the walls were broken, the walls were down.

I must not claim too much here. The divisions of the world were still there, but there in that place for that brief epiphany, they were down. While I could never be grateful for all the pain and suffering Steve went through in his addictions, I was nonetheless struck with the people he had brought into our lives. To be glad in grief is a torque of human emotion that requires devastating loss and the advent of an Unexpected Gift beyond our powers of anticipation. In the rupture of his death came these sinews of people bridging the torn separations of Steve's loss.

Steve had asked to be cremated. That past summer he and Nancy were out on the lake where we lived. As they were talking, he said, "If I ever crash, I want to be cremated and I want my ashes spread here on Lake Waukomis." He was well acquainted with the dangers of motorcycles, and maybe he had a premonition. He had said this after he had dried out, and we took him seriously.

So the morning after the wake our family and Gene and Sarah Lowry went to the crematorium. The man there told us that people did not usually come to these things. We told him that Steve would not take this last step without us. His brother Shawn and I had also talked, and we decided that we would push the body into the crematorium. We believed that Steve would want us to make this move and not someone he did not know. Besides we were going to do this with him.

Our friend Gene Lowry did the committal service before we pushed Steve into the crematorium. I remember the one thing that provided such clarity to the moment. Gene simply said, "Shit happens." He decidedly did not even suggest that Steve's death was God's will, but actively opposed such a notion. It was a powerful, healing moment.

After a prayer the time came, and Shawn and I got behind the large cardboard box in which Steve's body had been placed. It had a wooden support structure for strength. As we pushed, it became stuck about halfway in. Shawn and I looked at each other and smiled, seemingly seeing this situation the same way. One of us said something like, "Well, he never would let anyone push him around before, why start now?" We both quietly chuckled through our tears, but finally he went. As the box fully entered the furnace, the drape over it fell at Steve's feet, and one uncovered foot wobbled from side to side, a macabre gesture of the finality of what we were doing.

As we left the crematorium that morning, we did not look back, but the Lowrys did. They said as we left that the furnace fired up and the smoke from the chimney seemed to follow after us. It seemed to go west on Truman Road. Surely it had only to do with the way the wind was blowing that day, and surely it was just chance that it did. Surely. . . .

At the funeral that afternoon the chapel was packed. As agreed the Visions Motorcycle Club filled the first three rows on the right side of the room across from our family on the left. The remainder of the chapel was filled with that strange assortment from the night before, only more so. Around the walls of the chapel were others of Steve's friends, young men with sleeveless shirts and big tattoos wearing jeans and boots whose bearing bore an uncomfortable sense of where they were but a determined grit to be there in honor of Steve.

The first hymn was "Hope of the World." I remember so wanting to sing. I wanted to shout the affirmations of that song, but I was choked with grief even as I was filled with its claims of hope. But those in the chapel boomed it with their voices and in the last verse spoke the word that blinded me with tears and reduced my voice to a mere mouthing of what I could only wish I could shout.

> Hope of the world, O Christ o'er death victorious,
> who by this sign [the cross] didst conquer grief and pain,
> we would be faithful to thy gospel glorious;
> thou art our Lord! Thou dost forever reign.[1]

The biblical readings embodied the group. Bishop W. T. Handy, Jr., read the lesson from Philippians 4:4-7, the passage about the peace that passes understanding. Our pastor, Bill O'Quinn, read the Psalm, "God is our refuge and strength," and a woman who was a member of Visions read Isaiah 40:28-31. She said "Those of us who know Steve know how fitting this is about him."

> Have you not known? Have you not heard?
> The LORD is the everlasting God,
>   the Creator of the ends of the earth.
> He does not faint or grow weary;
>   his understanding is unsearchable.
> He gives power to the faint,
>   and strengthens the powerless.
> Even youths will faint and be weary,
>   and the young will fall exhausted;
> but those who wait for the LORD shall renew their strength,
>   they shall mount up with wings like eagles,
> they shall run and not be weary,
>   they shall walk and not faint.

---

1. HOPE OF THE WORLD
   by Georgia Harkness
   © 1954, Ren. 1982 The Hymn Society (admin. Hope Publishing Company, Carol Stream, IL 60188). All rights reserved. Used by permission.

Neil Blair, a former student of mine who had become a good friend of Steve's did one of the eulogies. He asked rhetorically: "Have you ever known anybody like Steve in your lifetime? Not in my lifetime. Have you ever loved anybody like him? Not in my lifetime." Steve reminded Neil of the little girl in the nursery rhyme with the curl in the middle of her forehead: when she was good, she was very good; when she was bad, she was very bad. He told the story of the time Steve was almost killed by electro shock. Later when Steve was asked how he survived it, he answered, "God didn't want me, and the devil was afraid I would take over!"

Neil spoke of Steve's fierce intensity, of his hates and loves, of the good and bad in his life. He did not duck the realities of Steve's siege of addiction or of his pushing the edges of every situation in which he found himself. He said of Steve that if there were fifteen rails protecting travelers on a road above a cliff, Steve would be out on the fifteenth rail walking on the very edge of the precipice. "He always walked the edge, and the edge would be a fence. . . . In twenty-nine years he may have just lived more than all of us by understanding top-rail walking."

In his concluding words Neil reflected on the last nine months of Steve's life when he got sober, when he turned his life over to God, when he came to accept himself, when he became free to live, and by that free to die.

There were then comments from the congregation. Honda Bob, Steve's good friend from Visions, spoke of his anger at God. Another young man who met Steve in a program of recovery spoke of growing to love him. "I watched his attitude go from

'I'm gonna rip some guy's head off and throw it across the street' to 'I'm gonna pray for him.'" In Steve's reaching out to people with chemical dependencies the young man said, "He would go places where nobody else would go." A staff person at the Kansas Community Center where Steve had gone to dry out, told her "favorite Steve story." While in detox she advised Steve to "find a new playground and new playmates to stay sober." Steve wondered out loud where a guy like him would find people who loved motorcycles who would let him be a member. He came in one day to the center and said he had found Visions. She asked, "Where are they?" "I don't know, they won't tell me!" Visions had a probation period, and Steve had to work his way in. She then spoke of how many people Steve had helped in the last months of his life.

Steve's brother, Shawn, spoke of all the fights they had had, "most of which Steve had won." He observed "Steve was right out on the edge for a long time and being with him was exciting." He then added, "Steve isn't gone. He's gonna be with me the rest of my life. I'm gonna miss his physical presence, but he'll be by my side. Nothing else has ever separated us. This won't either."

The eight-year-old daughter of one of the Visions couples went to the mike. She had written a poem for Steve that morning. Part of it said:

> Today is a good time and a bad time too,
> Cause you'll be an angel in an hour or two
> We're sorry you have to go
> But you're going the way you want to.
> Hey, at least you went sober and not drunk!

Glen Wiggs, a former pastor of ours, then told the story of the time Steve had come to see him. He had been pulled over for speeding in a thirty-five-mile-an-hour zone. Glen opined to Steve that a lot of people get pulled over for speeding in that community. "Yeah," answered Steve, "but I was riding my bicycle!"

Gene Lowry did the other eulogy:

> We all have to be acutely aware that we gather as stricken companions caught in a whirlwind of grief and pain. Underneath it all is the question of why? Why now? Why? The question is inevitable; it is inescapable. Why? The trouble is the heart raises questions that the mind cannot supply. I simply have to say that it is better to live with our questions unanswered than to be content with answers that will not do, will not sustain, will not empower.
>
> Because, of course, the question is unavoidable; we forget something about the question itself and that is that the question *why* has an answer built in. Because when you ask the question "why?" the assumption is that there is an answer, and that is an assumption. We are tempted to wonder, worry, think about, consider some special providential purpose, some divine mandate, that has cause that lies behind this moment of grief. I say, if we finally resolve to some sort of answer, to some hidden purpose we have to adjust ourselves to, then we will malign the very character of a caring God, a God who weeps when we weep and who suffers when we suffer. I want to say, clearly, that in my view we have come together this day by accident. And we are confronted by the larger mystery of life and death, and the larger mystery is not why we die, but how is it that we ever lived?

The final hymn was "Amazing Grace." The lyrics had been written by John Newton after his conversion. He had been a slave trader before coming to faith. There is gravity, then, when he writes "Amazing grace! How sweet the sound that saved a wretch like me!" It seemed so to fit the wretched way Steve came to see himself before sobriety. In the singing the congregation virtually shouted the hope of that song. I felt lifted and carried. I had come to terms with the fact that, choked with emotion, I could not sing; so I placed myself in the power of that song, of the singing of that congregation. Before the fifth verse the organist modulated up to the next key and the words swelled and washed over us:

> Yea, when this flesh and heart shall fail,
>   and mortal life shall cease,
> I shall possess, within the veil,
>   a life of joy and peace.

At the wake one of the Visions team members told us of their tradition of concluding their meetings with the Lord's Prayer. He indicated that they always put their arms around each other. So after the hymn the Visions team led us in the Lord's Prayer. That strange mix of people gathered up in each other's arms and prayed, and at the conclusion the Visions members shouted as they always did: "Keep coming back!"

After the service we got in the car with Steve's ashes and headed toward home and Lake Waukomis. Going down Truman Road I looked in the rear viewmirror and behind us must have been thirty motorcycles riding two by two. All the way home we led this funeral procession. They had gotten word of the site of the spreading of the ashes, and they were coming. So we went: we the family in our red van, and they the Visions on their freshly clean motorcycles and in their finest leathers and boots.

At home our neighbor, Barry Tedford, got his pontoon boat out and told us he would drive for the spreading of the ashes on the lake. He and Steve so loved each other that he seemed like a godsend. We went about fifty feet off the shore in front of our house. The ashes were in a brown rectangular box. I removed the lid and looked back at the bank. There the Visions were standing in an "at rest" military-like position up and down some forty yards of the shoreline. Peggy, Shawn, and Jennifer gathered with me at the side of the boat. The granular and dusty white ashes began their soft fall into the water seeming to flow with the words: "Into your hands, O God, we commend Steven Sample. . . ."

2

EVIL

In his midthirties Tom T. Burns was a rising young businessman in my community. Articulate, funny, personable, and engaging, I enjoyed his presence and admired him, identifying him as one I wished I could be like. He was tall and weighed in at about two-hundred pounds, I guessed, and had these huge hands. Adept but polite, he met people well and was liked by everyone I knew in my town. I was about fifteen, and in my adolescent eyes he could do no wrong.

So I was thrilled when he pulled up in my front yard one day and asked if I would like to go with him to do a little business.

"You need to learn about insurance, Tex, and this will be a good introduction for you." I was delighted, not because I had interest in insurance, but because he would choose me to be a part of one of his transactions.

"I've got to go across town and make this payment on a life insurance policy. It will be good for you to see how business is done," he informed me as I got in the car. We drove east on

Monticello Avenue across the business district and took a left on Second Avenue. When we took the third right I realized we were going into what was known as the "quarters," that part of town where "the colored people" lived. We went a couple of blocks, and he pulled over on the side of the road opposite three shotgun houses. "Come on, I want you to go with me," he said. I got out, and we crossed the narrow gravel road and then balanced our way across a two-board-wide, homemade bridge that crossed the ditch in front of one of the shotgun houses.

I knew, of course, that we were going in the home of "a colored family," but I was not prepared for what was inside. As soon as I entered the door, I saw black people sitting all around the walls in this small room. On three sides of the room, there must have been a dozen people sitting on wooden chairs and stools. On the west wall was an open casket with an old man lying in it. At the foot of his casket sat an old woman, who I learned was his wife.

Mr. Burns moved toward her, shook her hand, and said, "I am sure sorry about your husband, Auntie, you have my real sympathy." He then motioned to me to come over and shake her hand, which I did with no little formality, bending at my hips, and bowing. Then not knowing what to do next, I just stepped back to the middle of the room. Someone offered Mr. Burns a chair next to the widow, and he sat down. I continued to stand.

"Auntie, I know this must be a hard time for you. These things are so hard."

"Yassir, Mr. Burns, it is a mighty bad time. We had been married forty-six years this past May."

"Well, Auntie, I'm here to help you out in this bad time," Mr. Burns offered. "Auntie, I've got your husband's insurance money with me in cash. That will help you out a whole lot." With that he reached in his pocket and pulled out $600 in ten- and twenty-dollar bills. It looked huge and was probably more money than the people in that room had ever seen.

"Yassir, it will; we do have a lot of bills."

"Auntie, do you remember that your husband did not want to buy this life insurance? You remember he thought he didn't need it."

"Yassir, Mr. Burns, I do remember that."

"I'll bet you are really glad he bought that insurance now, aren't you."

"Yassir, I am."

"Well, Auntie, I have something here that will help you and your family *now*. I have here with me a life insurance policy on you that can be paid up in full for just $300. That will leave you the other half to pay for his funeral and help you with your bills."

"Well, I appreciate that, Mr. Burns, but we really needs that money."

I stood there and agreed with her. She did need that money, but Mr. Burns interrupted:

"Auntie, that's just what your husband said when I first tried to sell him this insurance policy. But you are awfully glad now that I did aren't you?"

"Yassir, I am, but Mr. Burns we really needs that money."

"Auntie, I have the cash right here. I have a receipt here that you can sign for the money, and I have a new policy right here. All you have to do is make your mark on these two pieces of paper, and you are all fixed up."

"Mr. Burns, I know you tryin' to help me and I appreciate that, but we just really needs that money." She was choosing her words carefully, trying not to anger Mr. Burns, trying to sound appreciative. I felt sorry for her and wanted to get out of there. I was hoping that Mr. Burns would take her answer as a "no" and accept it as such. It was not to be.

Mr. Burns then raised his voice and spoke with an edge in it. For the first time he let his anger show through.

"Auntie, I am trying to help you, and I don't think you understand what we're doing here. I said you should buy this new insurance policy paid in full. Do you understand what I am saying?"

She realized that she had to do what he said just to get half the money. I supposed that he could walk out the door with all of that money and then come up with delays and technicalities to keep her from getting it, at least right away, and maybe never.

"Yassir, Mr. Burns, give me the papers." He handed her first the new insurance contract and showed her where to make her mark. She then turned and placed the paper on the foot of her husband's casket and signed her X. The scratching of the X sounded like a muffled scream. He then handed her the receipt for half the insurance money on which she also made her mark. Mr. Burns then counted out $300 in twenties on the foot of the casket.

The biting contradiction of her signing away her husband's legacy on his casket bloodied the room. It was not mere thievery but an amputation on his last gift to her. It was a dismemberment scarred even more severely by forced but legal consent to humiliating transgression.

The faces in the room looked straight ahead in some kind of impassive countenance. They gave no hint of what they thought or what was transpiring in the room. They seemed practiced at such things. I stood there looking at the floor. I knew perfectly well that something terribly wrong was being done. In those years I had not been exposed to the civil rights movement. I had not read in the field of black and white relationships as I would later. I was a typical white teenager in South Mississippi, but I knew this was wrong.

At that point something mystical happened. The room took on the quality of night. I don't mean the light in the room changed, but it "darkened." It was a lit room devoid of light. I felt as though I were in a void, not one of a deep relatedness, but one of vast separation and searing judgment. I sensed an unbridgeable gulf between Mr. Burns and me, on the one side, and the black people in that room, on the other. This was especially so with the widow whose name I never knew. What happened in that room took no more than a few minutes, but it had the interminability of a long night of pain. The void was the hollowing out of my moral integrity.

The event had a tactile quality. I could feel the people in the room on my skin. It was as though in the separation and alienation of those moments moral demand took on an embodied tangible cast. The claims of a simple justice pulled at the very surface of my body, and I in frozen complicity stood there. The moral obligation in the room took on an ecological character, but my courage shriveled.

I wanted to stop it, and I could have if I had just started shouting at Mr. Burns. I could have broken up this "transaction" if I had made a scene and expressed my moral disgust at what he was doing. But such an action seemed beyond the world I was in. It was no part of the reality I knew. Maybe that's not quite it. I had this sense that I did not know what would happen next if I crossed that line. I had never seen that done. I do remember the contradiction, feeling that, on the one hand, I could stop it and, on the other, that the world would simply end or disintegrate. I felt, as cowardly as it was, that I would be flailing against the very nature of the world and that I had no idea of where things would go after that. I don't mean to justify my silence. Rather I simply want to convey what went on with me in those minutes.

I am not aware of saints or others reporting mystical events as judgment, but that day such was my experience. It is a void. It is an expanse. It is encompassing. It seems infinite in space and time. But it is a void of condemnation and an expanse of moral exactions unanswered and unmet. It is encompassing, but it is an environment of failed conscience. It may not be finally infinite in space and time, but its ongoing consequences and its capacity for harm run to lengths not predictable.

Some people try to excuse me from my role in that event. They say I was just a young kid, who did not know the gravity of what was going on or could not be expected to take a stand in circumstances like that. It won't wash. I knew exactly what was happening, and I knew without question that it was wrong.

I do apologize that my account addresses my experience and not the fate of the widow after this signing away of her inheritance. I don't know what happened to her. I cannot imagine that she was able to do much more than pay off her husband's funeral. Probably a domestic or at least working for white people, she in all likelihood lived the rest of her life in poverty. Not that an additional three hundred dollars would have changed all that; but it would have helped and, besides, it was rightfully hers, and she was clearly coerced to give it up.

We left the house within minutes. Mr. Burns again expressed his sympathies and said, "Believe me, Auntie, you made a wise decision today, and you will be glad you did it."

Back in the car, moral pain roared in my body. I finally said, "Mr. Burns, that was wrong. That just ain't right."

"Boy, you just don't understand business."

"She needed that money."

"That ole nigger woman would have just thrown that extra money away," he replied.

As we drove back to Second Avenue and back to my house, I doubted that that woman ever wasted anything in her entire life. But I made my protest too little and too late.

3

THE SYRUP CAN

We were the pipe-pulling crew for a seismograph operation in Pike County, Mississippi. I was eighteen, having just finished high school and working to pay my tuition to college the coming fall. He was African American, and I will call him Jim. About thirty-five or so, he was poor and making along with me seventy-five cents an hour. Illiterate with little, if any, schooling, he knew a lot more about the oil field and just work in general than I did, but I was white and he was black. So I was "the trucker," the boss of the rig, and he was the swamper, the helper who took orders from me.

Seismograph crews travel around an area and drill shallow holes. In our area, they were 240 to 280 feet deep. They then run dynamite down into those holes and explode it. These crews have tech instruments to trace the reverberations of the explosions on rock formations deep in the earth. Since they can identify rock formations where oil is more likely to be found, seismograph crews are central to the exploration for black gold.

The pipe-pulling crew follows along behind the seismograph operation several days later and pulls up the pipe to salvage as many joints as possible. These pipes are four inches in diameter and about ten feet long, so they are valuable and can be reused again and again unless burst or blown apart by the explosions. We usually could save ten or twelve joints per hole.

We had an A-frame truck that rode rough as hell and required a lot of steering. Later that year when I was at LSU I believed that I had gained considerable forearm strength from wrestling the steering wheel on that wayward machine. The truck was called an A-frame because of the upside down V on the back of the truck bed: two pipes coming together from each back corner of the truck to an apex about twelve feet off the ground. Hanging from this apex was a sizeable pulley through which ran a motorized winch line that I operated with three levers at the rear of the truck bed. We dropped the winch line around the end of the pipe sticking out of the ground and pulled it up. We then unscrewed it, threw it on the truck, and pulled up another. The swamper used a thirty-six wrench to break loose the pipe, sometimes using a cheater bar, that is, a pipe longer than the wrench that you could fit over the pipe and thus get more leverage.

This sounds easier than it is. For one thing, the drill site had a slush pit, two holes in the ground about a yard square each and about two feet deep. When the seismograph crew drilled, it would make slush in the pits. This slush was then pumped down through the pipes. Not only did it cool the drilling bit, but it would push the sludge out of the hole and clear the way for more drilling. This sludge was then deposited into these slush pits. What you did in effect was to cycle the sludge in and out of the hole. The problem for the pipe-pulling crew is that the whole time you work, you try not to step into that slush pit, which at times required no little agility.

More than that, the pipes were often hard to pull up. I would jerk the winch trying to break them loose, but that did not always work. The winch would sometimes pick the front end of the truck up off the ground. We were told not to, but the only way sometimes to break loose the pipe was to go around to the front of the truck, stand on the bumper, and bounce the front end to try to free the pipe. This was a good way to break ribs if the truck fell and threw you on the hood.

Sometimes, too, the pipes were hard to break loose from each other. Often, it took both of us on the cheater bar pulling with all our strength to unscrew a pipe. Further, we were working in ninety-plus degree, humid weather. To add to the problem these holes often seemed located in stifling places: an opening in a wooded lot, down in a close hollow, or just out in an open field where the sun bore down with relentless, oppressive heat.

Jim and I had worked together for about a month when we showed up at the gas station where we parked the truck over night, since we were working away from the home office. That morning someone had stolen the water can off the truck, something that seemed to happen often. I made an "executive decision" that we would just head off to the eastern part of the county without a water can. I said, "There will be plenty of stores where we can get water and cold drinks."

Without saying a word Jim went around back of the gas station and returned with a rusty syrup can. He filled it with tepid water from the faucet by the gas pumps and set it down between his feet. I looked over to see this water with flecks of rust in it, and the swirl of an oily stain floating across the top. Inwardly I gloated that Jim would make do with such a contaminated substitute. I felt a decided superiority.

We drove fifteen miles to the first hole. Arriving about seven-thirty, we found the location in an opening of pines. The night before had not cooled, and the morning sun was already weighing in on this break in the trees. We dropped the winch line over the top of the first pipe and yanked it up. Jim slapped a wrench on it and pulled. It did not budge. So we both got on the cheater bar. Jim and I both yanked on that cheater bar and sweated through our shirts in the first fifteen minutes. I cursed the fact that the drilling seemed to have welded those pipes together.

It took almost an hour to get twelve pipes out of that hole. We were both wringing wet with perspiration. Already my mouth seemed full of cotton balls. I was sucking on my tongue to get spit. We climbed back in the truck. Jim picked up that can of water, blew the rust flecks and the oily stain back, and took a long slow drink. Never looking at me, he stared straight ahead. As a black man in that world he hid any gloat there might have been. Meanwhile, I tried to look self-sufficient. When we got back on the road, I knew there would be a country store; and I began to imagine an orange soda or an RC Cola.

Within a half mile we came to the ribbons on the barbed wire fence designating where a gap entrance had been made to the next hole. Jim opened the gap, and we went through it. Headed down hill, I realized we were heading into a wetland. While the hole was not in the water, it was within thirty feet and to get around some trees we had to go part way through a swamp. The truck got stuck, and we had to get the winch line and literally winch ourselves from one tree to the next just to get to the hole. I hated that damned hole and that asthmatic truck. Needless to say, we were already exhausted by the time we got to the hole.

The morning sun was up and breathing fire. The swamp only made it a sauna. We got fifteen pipes out of that hole. While they were not so hard to break loose, it only meant we therefore were working faster. I remember trying to forget my thirst, trying to focus on pulling the pipe, trying to keep up my end of the bargain. I was not about to let Jim outwork me. I wanted to show him that I didn't need water, at least not yet. Besides, I kept telling myself, I am an athlete. I have pitched in hotter weather. I can do this.

By the time we winched the truck back out of the hole, I was trembling and getting a headache. At times I could not tell whether my vision was blurring or that I just had sweat in my eyes. I knew enough to know the dangers of heat stroke, and I knew I had to have water. It was now ten o'clock, two and a half hours of work without fluids of any kind. In fact, I had not had anything to drink since breakfast early that morning.

Jim opened the gap to let me through and closed it behind me. Getting in the truck he reached down and picked up that syrup can and gulped down a third of it, again looking straight ahead. He did not say a word. He just sat there looking at the road piecing its way through the snake turns of a pine forest. Having lost hope in finding a store in this godforsaken rural back-water, I was looking for a creek, or some small branch, anything with water in it. My hopes were dashed a few hundred yards down the road when we came to another marked gap in a barbed wire fence.

In denial, I knew I was fine. I can do one more. No problem. I put my bare arm down on the truck window and jerked it away. The late morning sun was like a blowtorch wilting what it did not burn. We drove into this field. I reassured myself that at least there was not a swamp. There was no shade either. We had to back up the truck at a good angle to the hole because that was a large slush pit. We dropped the line and began pulling pipe. They stuck. The winch line pulled the front of the truck three feet off the ground. We went there, stood on the bumper, and jumped up and down. The pipe finally broke loose and threw me down on the truck hood.

I was feeling woozy and exhausted. We went to work pulling pipe. It went well but it went fast and kept me working without a break. My headache was getting worse. My coordination was not good. I stepped off into the slush pit up to my knee, and had to pull myself up. Jim was bathed in sweat, and I noticed that I was not sweating much at all, yet I was burning up. I knew just enough about heat stroke to know I was in trouble. Somehow I made it through that pipe-pulling session and we crawled back in the truck. I could tell Jim was watching me and knew I was in danger. In all likelihood he was far more conversant than I with working without adequate food or water. He again reached for the syrup can and took a long slow draw.

I had to have water, but I was a white boy who had never knowingly drunk from the same glass or anything else with a black person. My own racism was actively at work in my head, but I needed water more than I needed prejudicial prohibitions.

"Uh, Jim, could I . . . can I . . . would you mind if I . . . uh . . . had . . . a . . . drink from your can?"

"No, suh, Boss, help yo'self."

With that he handed me the syrup can, and again looked straight ahead. My hands were trembling from dehydration and overexertion as I took the can, and when I looked into the bottom of it, it had rust flakes and a heavier film. But it looked like the finest vessel of water I had ever seen. I drank and did not mind the grit that came with the last couple of inches of water.

As I drank, it hit me. "This is the cup of salvation given for you." I had been going to church since I was about ten years old, and my church only celebrated Holy Communion about once a month. So I was not that formed by the practice of the Lord's Supper, and yet, I so distinctly remember the sense that I was being served Communion. In my stark need Jim became a priest to me, and I felt that I was being given life, and in a very literal sense I was. That syrup can became a chalice, and that hot water, permeated with rust, compromised with grit and topped with a greasy-looking film became the blood of Christ.

Anyone reading this should have questions about the integrity of this event. I certainly never knew Jim's feelings about what was going on. I did thank him and said something about how stupid I was to come off without water and that we would go and get some before we did anything else. But I did not know how to say anything more. I can imagine that he must have seen the irony of this arrogant white kid who thought he could work in such heat without water. I doubt that he missed the fact that a white boy still in his teens who would not typically eat or drink with him in his home was more than willing to share the same can of water when his life depended on it. I say this knowing that there were whites and blacks who ate together in the South in those spaces where such things did happen occasionally, but this had not been my experience.

I have no reason to believe that Jim saw this as Communion. What he thought I will never know. In a very real sense all I had was the reality of that syrup can. My pretensions of racial superiority were crashing on the sheer rocks of my abject need.

That syrup can became more important than skin color, socialization, and segregation. To be sure, there were walls of separation between us. He had his education in the hard knocks of race and class, and mine came in a good high school with resources. We lived in a segregated world where he knew stifling oppression and I, though not the offspring of an affluent family, knew privilege he would never know. As closely as we worked together, sometimes body to body pulling on that cheater bar with all our strength, we labored nevertheless in a world of walls. At the end of the work day we went to radically different homes and radically different lives.

If I were someone else reading this, I would likely not believe what I say next, but in my mind I knew that that syrup can stood on top of those walls and called them into question. I certainly could not say then what the Eucharist later came to be for me, but there was something about the reality of that shared syrup can that shifted my sensibilities. It was more than an attitude adjustment. A connection between the Lord's Supper and racial walls of separation was clear to me. It would take me some time to learn to say that better, but Robert Frost said that there is something that does not love a wall. It is a syrup can chalice. I drove the truck back through the gap, and we sped ten miles to a store we knew. We got plenty of water and under a tree outside the store, we broke bread together.

4

13 TAXI

Thirteen Taxi," I answered. "Yes, please send a cab to 546 West Congress Street." "I'll do so right away," I answered, trying to sound older than I was.

At twelve years of age I began to help Daddy and Momma by being the "dispatcher" at the cabstand. I was old enough to answer the phone, write down addresses, and give them to the drivers. I would not start driving the cabs until I was sixteen when I could get a commercial driver's license in Mississippi. I had no idea what an impact the cabstand would have on my life and that I would spend no little part of the rest of my life trying to understand it.

The cabstand got its name from its phone number which was 13. In those days there were no dial or punch-button phones, and in my town the phone numbers were only two or three digits long. You picked up the phone, the operator came on the line to ask "Number please?" and you just said "13." That got our line.

Later Daddy bought the Yellow Cab franchise and changed the name accordingly, but with only four or five cars, that sounded exalted to me. I preferred 13 Taxi.

The cab business was our entrance into the lower-middle class. During the Great Depression, Dad worked three jobs as an ice man, a shoe cobbler, and a school-bus driver. When World War II began, he went to work in the shipbuilding yards of New Orleans. There as a sheet and metal worker he helped build landing vessels for the war effort. When the war ended, he had put together enough money to make himself eligible for the necessary loan to buy the cab company. Suddenly Momma and Daddy were owners of a business.

When they bought it, the "cabstand" consisted of four beat-up cars and a telephone box in a café. By the time I began answering the phone, we had rented a twelve-foot-by-twelve-foot brick building next to Mr. Perkins's furniture store. I did not realize at the time that, except for sleeping and school, I would spend more time in that cabstand during those six years than any other single place in the world.

Everyday life in a cabstand is the story of an ongoing procession of characters. The names of the drivers, for one thing, bespeak the utter singularity of each one of them. Names like Luke Lee, Deroy Watts, and Coal Oil Jordan only begin a litany of remembrance. They populate my memories like cornstalks in a July field. But there were others equally memorable who just liked to hang out there. The editor and publisher of the local newspaper, two partners of a construction company, a local photographer who ran his own pornographic business in town, and, of course, a long line of inebriated men and some women who came in there falling down drunk. It often fell to me to "entertain" them when I was not trying to keep the drunks from beating me up.

A cabstand is a strategic place from which to see a small town. You see the underbelly of a community. You see people, often very respectable people, in heavily compromised moral situations. You find out what people do in the back stages of their lives. One night a driver called me from the stand to come out to the car so he could tell me that he was going to McComb, a town about twenty-five miles away. When I ran up to the car, I stuck my head in the window and saw a woman in the backseat, a very respected woman in town, sitting between two men, neither of whom was her husband. From the smells and the disheveled look of the three of them, I realized I had looked in on what the cabdrivers jokingly called a "ménage a twot." I would later understand that the driver and the two men were taking her to a hotel in another town for a more extended "visit."

My favorite cabdriver at 13 Taxi was Jay. He had a good build; and, though fully bald, he was a handsome man. He wore dress slacks, silky shirts unbuttoned to the waist, and used Mennen shaving lotion. Such things distinguished him from other drivers who dressed in a cheaper and more utilitarian fashion. Jay also loved music and had a sense of humor about it. Taking a soft-drink bottle, he would play it like a jug. He played one blues piece over and over again, along with country music tunes he loved. All I have to do is think of him to "hear" that blues tune and those solos on that bottle.

Women loved him, and I noticed how many of them asked for Jay when calling for a cab. He maintained a relationship with about a dozen females in that town, and I, though in my middle teens with my hormones boiling, wondered how on earth he could not only initiate so many liaisons but also manage to stay "current" with them all. A local freelance photographer who did porno on the side, used Jay as his chief model, primarily because Jay was so well-endowed and also because he had no trouble getting females to work with him.

Jay also scared me. His anger boiled just below the surface. It had a hot, scalding character that I did not want turned in my direction. Nothing could provoke his anger more or faster than some kind of slight, some indication that he was somehow less than others. When demeaned, his anger blazed into his face, and I can remember fantasizing that his face literally exploded. One day, one of our customers, usually a kind and considerate man, told Jay in a kind of offhand teasing way—certainly not meaning to insult Jay—that he would never be anything but a cabdriver because he had no ambition. I thought Jay would hit him, but he finally managed to laugh over his rage and turn it into a joke.

Now in his early thirties Jay was an intelligent man with no formal education to speak of. He had quit high school and had wandered from job to job until he started driving a cab. He worked with us for several years. Once he tried a stint in the

Army, but came home with four fingers on his left hand sawed off, the result of an "accident," he said; but he always added that it was "the quickest way out of the Army." Putting Jay in the Army was like putting a catfish in a glass of water, able to see the world, but in constraints more claustro-killing than burying him alive.

Then Jay met and fell in love with Margie, the owner of a small store on the wrong side of town. They became engaged, and all of a sudden his blues tunes turned to love songs and his country songs about "Born to Lose" became "I'd Waltz across Texas with You." He was a different man. He stopped his womanizing. His whole demeanor changed. The next two months were the happiest of his life.

I was at the cabstand the day Jay ordered the window fan—cash on delivery—for Margie's place. She lived in the back of her store, which got very hot during a Mississippi summer. The fan committed Jay to a fifty-dollar purchase, a great deal of money for a cabdriver in those days. He signed the order and gave off this big smile of satisfaction. He made some joke that implied that he and Margie would sensually enjoy that fan together on no few occasions.

Two weeks later when he returned early from an out-of-town cab trip, he stopped by Margie's store, went to her place in the back, and found her sexually engaged with another man. I never understood this violation of fidelity by Margie, especially since she planned to marry Jay. She was a smart person; everybody said so. I've wondered if she felt trapped in that small town. She lived on the wrong side of the tracks; and her store, while providing a living, was going nowhere. Some people said that the fastest way out of town was whiskey and sex, and Margie didn't drink.

The very next day, the goddamn fan came. The delivery post-man set the cardboard box down on the cabstand floor. Jay pulled out his wallet, took out and unfolded two twenty dollar bills and one ten, and reached into his pocket for postage. He gave it to the postman and for what was one very long minute stared at the package. Finally, he slowly opened the box, reached in and lifted out a heavy, large window fan, and set it on the floor. A tag wired to the fan flapped in the breeze, the only thing that moved in the room. Three of us—my father, myself, and Larry, a building con-tractor—sat watching. In such moments you want to yell out for someone to say the right thing, because you are terrified about what will happen next.

Breaking the silence Larry, knowing full well the context of all of this, offered, "I'll give you fifteen dollars for it." He then smiled this sickening smirk as if to gloat that he had his prey exactly where he wanted him. It was the cruelest thing of its kind I ever saw.

"You got it," Jay shot back in a "don't-give-a-damn" defiance not willing to be deterred by an offer so insensitive and heartless.

But my dad, in a move so typical of him, said, "I'll give you fifty dollars, Jay, plus postage." With that he went to the company purse, counted out the money, and gave it to Jay.

That was Wednesday. Jay seemed in another world. He played the soft-drink bottle, but he was not "on stage" as he usually was. He seemed caught in a trance. In these states he would sometimes smile, but it was a smile that frightened me more than his overt expressions of anger. It was a smile of such cynical resignation that one dared not intrude lest stepping on a landmine of fury so devastating that the explosion might destroy Jay and anyone with him.

That Friday evening I was driving all night, and Jay was working until midnight. There wasn't much business so Jay and I spent most of the time sitting on the porch of the cabstand just talking. He seemed more himself, more engaged. We talked of everything from my love of baseball to women and girls, from the cab business to time to get away from it all, from thoughts about things past to our hopes for the future. We had a long discussion about murder and suicide. The concluding comments just seemed too pedestrian, too insignificant.

"Tex, do you think you could ever murder somebody?"

"I dunno, Jay, I'm not sure I have ever been that mad at anybody. I sure hope I don't ever do that. I suppose in some rare situation or if I was crazy or somethin' I could."

"What about suicide? Could you ever kill yourself?"

"Well, I dunno about that either. I hope I'm never that down on myself. I think people who do that just really feel bad about things and about themselves. I hope I never get to that point."

"Yeah, me too. . . ."

With that he seemed to slide out of the conversation as though he just drifted away. We sat there watching the moon rise above the Illinois Central Railroad, just across the street. After a time we talked a bit more and about midnight Jay went home. Daddy relieved me around 5:00 the next morning.

I seemed to sleep hard for about three hours and then woke up around eight that morning. Unable to stay in bed, I went down town to help out by answering the phone. Jay was already back on the job and was out on a trip when I got there. I answered the phone a little after 9:30, and this voice in a whisper said, "Tex, your dad needs to get down here right away and get Jay's cab. It doesn't look good being here. Jay's shot and killed Margie, and he's shot hisself in the head. He ain't gonna live neither, they think."

Daddy flew out the door when I told him, and I heard the ambulance siren start up from King Daughter's Hospital. It raced by Mr. Perkins's furniture store within a half minute, went over past Panzica's Grocery, and turned south. Within fifteen minutes it came back wailing down Monticello Street. I ran to the corner of Mr. Perkins's store hoping to see Jay. In those days the ambulances were basically station wagons outfitted with a few medical instruments and a stretcher. The back windows had frosted lines across them to provide a modicum of privacy. As it raced by, I could only make out a large figure convulsing on the stretcher. It was Jay. He died fifteen minutes later at the hospital.

It came so blindingly fast. From that moonlit night of casual conversation just a few hours ago to this wholesale tragedy. The juxtaposition of these two events felt like a tearing apart of the body. It was a stark reversal of reality and emotion. I wondered then as I have a thousand times since why I did not see this thing coming. As I thought back through our conversation, I could hear things differently than I had the night before. Jay was reaching out to me. I don't think I felt guilt because I knew that all this was more than one conversation could have prevented. Though I don't need to deny some sense of guilt because in tragedy of this magnitude, the range of emotions and reactions are complicated. I knew even then that they were huge. Mostly I remember the missed opportunity. I had a chance, perhaps, to help Jay and by that Margie.

The night of the killings I went to bed struggling to comprehend the events of that day. The window fan had already been installed at our house the day before. Big azalea bushes covered the east windows of my room, and that fan pulled the cool air from the dirt around them. I lay there privileged by a fan central to the tragedy that had befallen our lives at 13 Taxi.

My head was filled with a thousand whys, and I could not help noticing the strange, quiet comfort of that fan whirling away from the kitchen at the back of the house. I could see Jay looking at the fan on the cabstand floor with the tag waving in the wind. The soft breeze that touched the tag seemed oblivious to the affront the fan brought, just as in our house it softly moaned in its dutiful labor so out of touch with all that had gone before. The fan that was to cool the passionate love of Margie and Jay was sold away into duty with my family instead. The cost of my comfort was whispered with a whirring repetition.

I did not blame us for having the fan. I admired my father for the way he stepped in and kept Larry from stealing the fan from Jay's wrath. Rather, it was the way that things did not come together, the way they stood in such contradiction. I thought Margie was happy and in love with Jay, and maybe she was!—all the more reason to question her infidelity. I wondered what this one-night stand in the afternoon was like, what it meant to her. Was it just sheer passion, or was it boredom looking for the day to pass? Was Margie looking for a quick way out of town, or was it the expression of an end to the relationship with Jay, a washout already known to her but still in the offing for him?

But then the question of how Jay, while loving her, could shoot her—five times he fired into the body he loved. In my mind I could "see" her jerking in shocked spasms each time he fired. I could then "see" Jay turn that pistol to his own temple. I could "see" that maniacal, furious shuddering rage of his and "hear" the sound of the pistol firing. As he collapsed to the floor beside her, I could "see" pools of blood edging toward each other and finding a cohabitation in death they could not consummate in life.

Why did love go so wrong? How did Jay miss this chance for something he so clearly longed for? Yes, Margie was wrong in her unfaithfulness to Jay, but why should she die for this? How could Jay go to such lethal lengths even in his devastated rage? I asked God why. I could not believe this was God's will, and certainly I do not now. But there was no answer. The silence of God filled that dark night. Only the fan drawing cool air from around the roots of azaleas made testimony, the Silence of an absent God drowned out by the whispers of a fifty-dollar fan, plus postage.

In the years since the deaths of Jay and Margie, I came to see God's Absence as some strange sense of divine Presence. While I don't doubt that God can choose an absence from us, there is a form of God's Presence we experience as Absence. I don't want to set myself up as privy to God's Absent Silence, but I often sense God's silence as a divine protest of the tragedy and evil in the world. It is a Silence like thunder, an Absence like relentless vicinity. Yet, the protest is so replete, and the Silence such a sonic void that even a window fan intrudes past the Absence and overwhelms the Silence.

I want to be gentle in comments about Jay and Margie. I wish not to judge them. Neither do I condone nor excuse their acts. They were people engaged in lives contrary to their gifts. Jay seemed like a left-handed man trying to write from the wrong side, Margie like an artist enslaved to a derelict store. They were stifled, not as in the closing off of breath, but the smothering of vocation and destiny.

With Margie I have never been able to get away from the claustrophobic character of her life. Perhaps it did not have the terror of being buried alive, but rather, the monotony of scenery that never changed and the suffocation of social constraint that operated like an asthma of soul. And Jay, the craziness about him seemed not his doing but rather something done to him. I wonder what he might have done, who he might have been, had he not been so possessed by demons that inhabited his mind with their libertine capacity to release floodgates of rage.

I now believe that the absence and silence of God on that night protested against the lethal powers that entrapped Margie and Jay in tragedy. Certainly it was a protest of the acts of Margie and Jay themselves, but even more it was a judgment of the larger powers that gripped our community and left people like Jay and Margie subject to lives they could not finally live.

Protest implies that the world is meant to be different. The world is not created for futility and death. It is not a place finally of cynicism and despair. The silence and absence of God point to a different destiny, a different aim for the world. Death, bondage, and alienation do not have the last word. The world does not end that way. In this strange and paradoxical sense, I see God's grieving, absent Silence as good news.

5

SANDWICHES AND KOOL-AID

On March 7, 1965, later known as "Bloody Sunday," a group of voting rights demonstrators led by Hosea Williams were violently attacked by police and state troopers near the Edmund Pettus Bridge in Selma, Alabama. Seventy African Americans were hospitalized and seventy more received treatment for injuries. This led two weeks later to a march from Selma to Montgomery led by Martin Luther King, Jr., to protest for voting rights. It would culminate at the state capitol in Montgomery on Thursday, March 25. Many describe this march as the very peak of the civil rights movement in its emotional and political impact. It led to the passage of the Voting Rights Act of 1965.

At the time I was a social action executive for the Massachusetts Council of Churches in Boston. My job the week of the march was to organize and to get airplane reservations for clergy and laity flying to Montgomery to join the effort. James Reeb, a Unitarian minister, was attacked on March 9 and died from his injuries March 12. His death only increased the passion of clergy and laity in Massachusetts to join the march.

The MCC chartered a commercial plane and flew about 200 clergy and laity down to join the march on Wednesday. We arrived at the campsite of the march in the early evening. We slept that night on an athletic field of the St. Jude's Catholic complex. I spent the night sleeping on my raincoat. It had rained earlier that day, but we were dry except for the wet ground.

The next morning Dr. King led some 25,000 of us out of the camp headed on the last leg to the state capitol, some seven miles away, as I remember. That crowd would grow as we marched to the capitol. Yet, along the line of the march were thousands of southern whites. A few made menacing gestures, most just looked at us grimly with disdain and anger, and the younger people more often just gave us the finger.

A decision had been made to take a jog and go through the black community as a show of support and solidarity. As we marched along, I saw the shotgun houses I had known all my life. There were dirt-bare yards around these houses where the grass had been rubbed off by too much humanity on too little space. Southern black poverty greeted us all along the march through the community.

Because I was tall and bigger than most, I was asked to walk on the outside of the march on the right side. Someone told me, "If somebody's gonna get hit, we would rather it be somebody your size." It was not a comforting thought, and I remember complaining to myself that demonstrators seemed to be terribly small.

As the morning wore on, I noticed the very humid spring of Alabama. My Mississippi blood had "thickened up"—as those New England Yankees would say—and, dressed in my Boston clothes, I began to feel the heat and to get quite hungry and thirsty. As inspired as I was to be there—and scared, I might add—I was nevertheless focused more on food and drink than anything else.

I looked up the line, and coming our way, that is, against the flow of the march, was a black woman. She had on a print dress that had endured many too many washings and well-worn shoes. She was very poor, I thought to myself. But in one hand she had a stack of peanut butter and jelly sandwiches and in the other a gallon jug of red Kool-Aid, strawberry as it turned out. I don't know why, but when she got to me, she shoved those sandwiches into one of my hands and that jug of Kool-Aid into the other. She then looked up at me and said, "Heah, Brother, we gonna overcome!"

I was dumbstruck. I uttered some kind of "Thank you," and looked down at the sandwiches and Kool-Aid. When I turned to say something else, she had disappeared into the crowd.

I took one of the sandwiches and passed the others to the person on my left. Cradling the plastic jug on my bent elbow while snaking my index finger through the handle, I lifted it above my head and took a long drink. I was proud that I knew how to drink from a jug. When I passed it on to that same man on my left, it hit me like a brick: "This is my body broken for you, and this is my blood shed for you." I chilled for the next quarter of a mile.

We continued the march down to the capitol and passed the Dexter Avenue Baptist Church, where King had pastored as he led the Montgomery bus boycott. Arriving at the capitol, we were the largest southern demonstration for civil rights in United States history. Once on the capitol grounds, we sat on the grass and watched and participated in the climax of what I experienced as a "liturgy" culminating a civil rights march. There were singers and other musicians; there were speeches and the introduction of dignitaries. We sang freedom songs and shouted support from where we sat. But we were all waiting for Dr. King to speak. We knew he would "bring it," and that would be the climax of the day, indeed of the entire march and the struggle that had preceded it in Selma.

Finally, after an introduction by Ralph Abernathy, King climbed to the back of a flatbed truck and began. The speech that day was as inspired and as powerful as his "I have a dream" speech in 1963 at the march on Washington. Throughout his compelling oratory, people black and white shouted support and encouragement. He spoke his dream: "Our aim must never be to defeat or humiliate the white man. We must come to see that the end we seek is a society at peace with itself, a society that can live with its conscience. That will be a day not of the white man, not of the black man. That will be the day of man as man."

Then he moved toward his conclusion. He knew great struggle still lay ahead, and he moved to the question of how long the dream would take.

"I come to say to you this afternoon however difficult the moment, however frustrating the hour, it will not be long, because no lie can live forever.

"How long? Not long, because you will reap what you sow.

"How long? Not long, because the arm of the moral universe is long, but it bends toward justice."

He then moved into a pattern of shouting "How long? not long; how long? not long." Then he seemed to shout to us: "How long!"

And that crowd of thousands upon thousands rose up off the ground and shouted in roaring response. "NOT LONG!" And he ended it with: "How long? Not long cause 'mine eyes have seen the glory of the coming of the Lord, trampling out the vintage where the grapes of wrath are stored. He has loosed the fateful lightning of his terrible swift sword. His truth is marching on. . . .' Oh, be swift, my soul, to answer Him. Be jubilant, my feet. Our God is marching on.

"Glory, glory hallelujah!

"Glory, glory hallelujah!

"Glory, glory hallelujah!"

At that point Dr. King had three years, three years before his body would be broken and his blood would be shed. With his death I would ask, "How long?" In the violence and wholesale injustice that continue to plague the earth, I have often asked, "How long?" But in all these things I can still hear that wonderful black woman with the peanut butter and jelly sandwiches and strawberry Kool-Aid, that wonderful celebrant of the Eucharist, speaking the word: "Heah, Brother, we gonna overcome!"

6

"PURDY"

In the eighth grade I had the world by the tail. I was on the fourth string of the high school football team (we were basically cannon fodder for the B team), I was the sports editor of the eight-grade newspaper, *Behind the Eight Ball*, and I was madly in love with a girl who in but three years would be the drum majorette of the Brookhaven High School Panther Band.

Then it began to happen. First, my feet went flat, and I had to get arch supports. Then my eyes went bad, and I had to get glasses. Then, I noticed these pains in my back, running down my leg. Every time I ran into one of those B-team players (notice I did not say "tackled," but just "ran into"), I felt this sharp sting. Some days my back would lock up, and I could hardly move. One day I was out playing in the yard, fell down with pain, and had a hard time getting up on my feet. I managed to get home to the bathroom and lay down on my back to ease the pain; but once I got down, I couldn't get up. I lay there waiting for someone to come home to help me. Unable to get off the floor and now scared, I lay there so long that I eventually lost control of my bodily functions and was a mess by the time Momma came back.

They took me to a "bone doctor." He said I had spondylolisthesis. The fancy word meant one of the vertebrae in my lower back was out of alignment. It sat forward. As a result it pinched nerves in my back and gave me pain. I don't know if the doctor was trying to scare me or just to get me to behave, but he told me that if I did not have surgery, I would "someday step off a curb and be paralyzed from my waist down," something that never happened.

He prescribed an armchair back brace that I would wear for the rest of the school year. I could come for an operation that summer. I asked what the surgery would do, and he said, "Basically, you will be a semi-invalid for the rest of your life" (also, something I never did). I then asked him about football, would I be able to play with the brace or the surgery? "Absolutely not," he said, "I'm sorry, young man, but football is over for you."

It seemed like the end of the world. Football meant everything to me. Johnny Lujack, the great quarterback at Notre Dame, was my hero; and I knew that I would someday go to that school and do what he had done. As far as I was concerned, he had defeated Doc Blanchard and Glenn Davis single-handedly in their gridiron battle of Notre Dame versus Army. This was before I found out that Notre Dame was Cath'lik, and that we did not go to their schools. But I was brokenhearted. I thought my life was over.

Then it got worse. I got acne. I don't mean a little acne. I had the best case of acne in south Mississippi. I could walk down the street, and people would hold up their index finger and shout

"He's Number 1!" Actually I might have been the best case of acne in all of Mississippi, but I never competed in the north.

This led to weekly trips to the dermatologist in Jackson, fifty miles away. My treatment consisted of shots directly into hardened cysts "to break them up," the doctor said. Then he used sulfuric acid to eliminate the formation of deeper scars. One wonderful result of this was a kind of rotten egg smell that I would try to cover with Old Spice shaving lotion. Finally, he did "burns" of dry ice designed to take off old skin and to replace it with new. For months I did these treatments every Saturday, then every other Saturday. They were simply torture.

What was worse was school come Monday. The shots made lumps, the acid made scabs, and the ice burns gave me a lobster-red skin. A few of the students, of course, "diagnosed" me with syphilis. Others asked: "Good God, what happened to you?" Perhaps the worst were those who pretended that the elephant—or the leprosy—was not in the room.

The problem with the face is that you can't hide it without wearing a mask. I learned how much your face precedes you into just about any situation. It is the first thing people see, at least most of the time. Eventually my friends and other students got more used to it, and they seemed to see it as just me. Meeting new people was hard. Most young people were kind. They would try to cover their reaction, which meant that their attempt to conceal their initial take was like an ice pick. It made not much of a physical wound on the outside, but it went deep and did damage. An unintended and covered revulsion is worse than an assault.

Of course, I lost my girlfriend to another football player. I certainly understood. Had the shoe been on the other foot, I doubt that I would have stuck with her. But really, in the hormone boil of junior-high crushes, you think at the beginning they are eternal. This one lasted as long as most, but under the circumstances the breakup was the last blow in an existential assault on what seemed to be my entire life.

That year Hank Williams began his brief but shooting-star flight across the heavens of country music, and my momma would wake us for school at 6:30 every morning with Hank on the radio. We heard that swamp panther voice of his wailing out "I'm So Lonesome I Could Cry." Mama would come into my room, put her hand on my chest, and gently shake me to wake me up. I was almost always already awake, but I did not let on. When my eyes finally opened, she looked at me and said, "You are so purdy."

You need to understand that in our world *purdy* was prettier than *pretty*, and to my momma I was purdy. So get this picture. I have flat feet, eyes that require glasses, a back with a brace, and acne from hair line to hair line, and my momma thinks I'm purdy!

I have no idea what would have happened to me if it had not been for my mother's sustaining love. I cannot remember a single time when she seemed put off by my condition. In my memory there is not one instance of her revulsion or of being ashamed of me. She was always a great kisser, and she continued that practice throughout that time and throughout her life.

When I turned fifteen, she and Dad bought me a used 1940 Ford Coupe. It cost $500 dollars. This came at a time when we had had several cab wrecks. Because of these wrecks the folks had to borrow money to keep the business going. Even so, they took out another loan to buy the coupe. The bank always lent them money because they knew they would pay it back. Talking to her one day, I told her that I knew they were not just broke but in debt. "Why in the world," I asked, "do you go out and borrow more money to buy me a car?" Her answer, "Son, you just need a car to go see the dermatologist in." With that she changed the subject. That's all I got from her at the time. I knew there was more.

It was twenty years before I got a straight answer. She stated, "Son, we were just so afraid you would run from life, and we wanted something that would keep you in the middle of the street." So it was a strange mix: fallen arches, bad eyes, a displaced vertebrae, acne, a Forty Ford Coupe, and a momma with no aesthetic sensibility whatsoever when it came to me. Most of these things were lethal to any sense of worth I might have, but Momma was clearly the saving ingredient. It would be years before I would see the connection between my mother's love and the grace of God.

The Ford only lasted a year or so. When I found out that they would *give* me burnt motor oil at the gas station, I quit buying new cans of oil and simply filled up the crank case with the used stuff. I figured it was a used car so used oil seemed fine. Besides, it burned so much oil that I figured it changed the oil itself every three tanks of gas or so. Don't misunderstand, the car was a great gift and did what it was supposed to do. The car got me into the middle of the street, but it was Momma that got me through.

7

AUNT BETSY

Brother Sample, do you make calls on people who aren't members of the church?" asked Miz Anna Rogers. She was a member at the New Canaan United Methodist Church where I was a student pastor. In my senior year of college I served New Canaan and three other churches on a forty mile string in South Mississippi. People in Mississippi didn't call you "Reverend" or "Pastor." They called you "Brother" or sometimes just "Preacher."

"Well, of course, I do," I responded with more largesse than I felt.

"Well, Aunt Betsy lives out here in the country about three miles, and she needs a preacher to come to call. She needs help."

"Miz Anna, I would be glad to call on her." I spoke with assurance trying to sound like a pastor who wanted to reach out to anyone.

"I'll go with you to show you the way and to make it all right. You see, the last preacher that went to see her she ran off with a butcher knife!" I tried to cover my reaction to this last bit of information. I'm sure I gulped, but I was committed.

My duties at the churches began on Saturday morning each weekend and lasted through an evening worship service on Sunday night. Saturday was my day to visit, so Miz Anna and I set a time to go.

I drove down that next Saturday from Millsaps College and picked Miz Anna up at her house. We snaked along a winding asphalt road through pine trees and blackjack oaks. Soon, Miz. Anna motioned to a house just up the road and asked me to pull over.

"You stay here, Brother Sample, I'll go up and make sure it's safe for you to come." She patted me on the knee to reassure me, opened the door, and headed up the path to this ramshackle of a house. Miz Anna, a woman in her fifties, was just about five feet tall, if that, and weighed maybe a hundred pounds. I was six-foot-three-and-a-half inches tall, weighed around a hundred and eighty pounds, and was a pitcher for my college. I did not miss the incongruity of this small woman protecting and taking care of me. I felt like a coward at the same time that I was relieved that she went ahead. She went in the door, stayed maybe a minute, came back out, and waved for me to come on. She looked like someone who had just dismantled a bomb and signaled it was now safe for me.

As I approached the house there were a couple of dogs, a few cats, maybe a half-dozen chickens, and a rooster. The door was on the side of the house, so I did not realize until I got almost in front of it that it had no screen and the wooden door was open. A chicken walked in ahead of me, and there was a cat and a dog already there. Going through the door, I sidestepped several piles of feces. These were the respective contributions from each of the critters who inhabited her yard, and quite apparently her house. She had to be the most thoroughly equal opportunity housing authority I would ever know, except for an occasional preacher she ran off with a rather long piece of cutlery.

Once I was inside, she came over with a slight hobble to greet me. In her eighties, she was on the heavy side and looked like a woman who had been quite beautiful in her youth. Her dress wore cereal from her breakfast that morning, and her makeup— applied in the time it took me to walk to the front door—went on over the traces of soot from the wood stove that sat near the middle of this one room house. I hated myself for noticing that dirt was caked between her fingers and around her neck.

"Oh, Brother Sample, I am so glad to meet you. Miz Anna says so many nice things about you." With that, she hugged me. I remember a strange mixture of scents. She was not hygienic, but my time in the cab business and in the oil field had prepared me for that. Still, I smelled this very strong shoe-polish odor. It stumped me. She picked up a pile of papers and odds and ends from a chair, and asked me to sit down.

I tried to look around the house without being too obvious. The floor was covered not only with animal waste but with trash and spills. It was a dirt floor that had not been swept or raked for weeks. Except for the chairs that she, Miz Anna, and I sat in, any other table, chair, or piece of furniture was covered in junk. It seemed she never threw anything away, and it was all *there*. The kitchen sink was filled with dirty dishes from a week or more. There was no indoor plumbing, and it struck me as odd that, except for a chamber pot almost under the bed, she was the only one of the "boarders" who went to the restroom outside.

As she began to talk, I noticed these bits of substance in her hair. They had a kind of dried out, crumbly character, and they were coal black. I then realized this substance was used to cover the gray in her hair. Shoe polish! I almost said it out loud. She colored her hair with shoe polish, black shoe polish. That's why I smelled it.

"Brother Sample, I know I ought to be going to church. I'm sorry I haven't even been yet to hear you preach."

"Well, we would love to have you come," I said. I meant it, but, I must say, I wondered what the reaction would be.

We talked for maybe thirty minutes, and I could tell that Aunt Betsy liked me, and Miz Anna was smiling with satisfaction. I sensed that Miz Anna's satisfaction was in great part the relief she felt that I was not run off at the point of Aunt Betsy's big butcher knife.

Once back in the car, Miz Anna started in almost immediately.

"Brother Sample, I hope you don't mind me bringing you out here, but as you see, she needs help. I'll tell you, she is just one of the saddest stories in this community. When she was young, she was the most beautiful woman in this county. She was just lovely and such a fine girl. When she married, she married the richest man in the county, and he just loved her to death. I mean, he worshiped the ground she walked on. But he took care of her completely. He never let her handle money. He never let her do things on her own. Don't misunderstand, he was awful good to her, but she just never learned anything about money or business or taking care of things. Well, he died in his early fifties, and she was just lost. She not only didn't know what to do with herself, she didn't know how to handle the property or their money or anything else.

"After he had been dead a couple of years, this handsome, fancy lookin' fellow came to the area and just swept her off her feet. He talked her into sellin' everything and headin' out west with him. So they took off. Well, she was back in six weeks, completely broke, and just lost. He had taken her for everything she had. She ain't never been the same since.

"You know, she has relatives in our church. Bob Collard is her grand nephew, but him and his wife, Mildred, just don't know what to do with her. They are ashamed of her and just worn out with trying to find some answers. You saw her on a good day, but she is kinda crazy."

After our visit Miz Anna started picking her up and bringing her to church. She was so pleased with the attention that she would sit out there with Miz Anna and listen to my sermons just transfixed. I'm not sure she really listened to what I said. I think she was just so glad to have a place in the community where she could come and be with a friend like Miz Anna.

After that, Aunt Betsy attended church regularly for about a month. One Saturday, however, when I arrived back at the church, I learned that Aunt Betsy had had an "incident."

Apparently she hiked six miles to a black juke joint, bellied down a good half-dozen beers and got herself falling-down drunk. The black folk at that juke joint did not feel they could deny her service and could not tell her "no" when she asked for more beer. Certainly they did not want any trouble over this white woman. So as soon as they could, they loaded her in the back of a pickup truck and took her home about midnight. I was told that she was standing on the bed of that truck just behind the cab and singing at the top of her voice the entire ride home.

That did it. In that world a white woman who went to a black juke joint and partied with black folk had to be crazy. Bob and Mildred and some other members of the family not in our church had her committed to the insane asylum near Jackson for "evaluation," but it was clear that the family hoped it was for good.

About six weeks later I got a call from the hospital.

"Reverend Sample, I'm an administrator for the hospital, and I need your help. We have a patient here who tells us that you are her pastor, and we need to release her, and we would appreciate it if you came by to pick her up and take her home."

"Sir, you need to call her family. I have the number. I can get it."

"Reverend," he stopped me, "we have called the family several times, and they refuse to come and get her. If someone doesn't come, we will just have to give her a bus ticket and send her home."

"Oh, please don't do that," I protested. "There is no telling where she might end up."

"We understand that, but legally we cannot keep her here, and she wants to leave. In fact, she says she wants you to come and get her."

"What did you find out her problem is?"

"According to our diagnosis she has an identity problem."

"What does that mean?"

"It means she doesn't know who she is."

After a few more efforts on my part to push the responsibility onto someone else, I finally agreed to pick her up that Saturday, which I did.

On Sunday, the next day, Miz Anna told me that neither she nor I was very popular with the family after bringing her back home. We did our best to explain the situation and hoped people would finally accept it. But it did not look good.

When I came down the next weekend, Miz Anna told me that folk were trying to freeze Aunt Betsy out. The store would not offer her credit even though she always paid. Her family would not have anything to do with her, and people in the community were basically ignoring her when they were not outright shunning her. Well, it pissed me off.

So that night I went to work on my sermon and basically "stole" a homily from a book I cannot remember. While I gave credit for where I got it, I made almost an outright "lift." The title of the sermon was "The Problem with Your Neighbor Is You." The basic idea was that if you have a problem with a neighbor in need, then the real problem is you, not the neighbor. I said that about six different ways in about twenty minutes. I am certain that I preached it with no little arrogance and self-righteousness. They probably should have just run me off. The reaction of the congregation, however, surprised me in that I did not get a lot of grief for the sermon. They just kind of filed out without comment. They spoke to me, but it was pretty much a formalism. I wondered if they even heard me.

When I arrived back in the community the next Saturday, I went first to see Miz Anna.

"Brother Sample, you won't believe what has happened. They have moved Aunt Betsy into another house, one up off the ground that's really nice and clean. They opened up a line of credit for her at the store so she can buy groceries, and they even told her she can buy cigarettes. Everybody just jumped in and gave her furniture and things from their houses so she could set up housekeeping with everything looking real good."

"That's wonderful. So, you think I'm going to get to keep my job and you are going to be able to stay in this community?" I only half joked.

"Oh, yes, these are good people around here. They just needed to be reminded who they are."

For the next three or four Sundays things rocked along very well. Aunt Betsy was there every Sunday. Fully attentive, she seemed to take in every word, and someone made sure she got to church.

About a month later, however, I was preaching away in the early spring of the year with the windows open. I began to notice a terrible smell. Pastureland came right up to the church, and barbed wire was actually nailed to the back of the building. Initially, I thought a cow had dumped near the church, and I simply tried to ignore it.

As I preached, though, I noticed that Miz Anna was whispering to Aunt Betsy with no little urgency. Miz Anna kept gesturing to Aunt Betsy to get up and go outside. Meanwhile Aunt Betsy was pointing at me and whispering loud enough that I could make out what she was saying: "Listen to the preacher. Listen to the preacher."

Miz Anna countered this by pointing to the aisle and urging her, "Let's go," all to no avail.

I then realized that Aunt Betsy had had no little stomach distress that morning and had had an accident of major proportions. I was so distracted that I doubt that I was coherent at all in my sermon, but I don't think anyone noticed because they were as otherwise engaged as I.

During the last hymn I walked to the back of the church to greet people as they left. I figured I had just as well take the flack then and there. I was sure that my tenure as the pastor was over.

Miz Anna somehow managed to get Aunt Betsy out with the first part of the crowd. If I had had any doubts about what had happened to her, it was totally clear when Aunt Betsy hugged me. Miz Anna followed her and spoke quietly but urgently to me, "Brother Sample, we have had it now. Do you know what Aunt Betsy just did in church?"

"Yes, I believe I do."

"I don't think we will survive this. This is just too much." With that she followed Aunt Betsy down the steps.

As the congregation filed out that morning, they looked grim and embarrassed. None relieved my anxiety about what would happen next.

One of the last people out the door was this BIG farmer. He was as tall as I but a half-foot wider and five inches deeper through the chest. When we shook hands, it seemed that his hairy paw completely engulfed mine, and I have big hands. He had a stern look on his face and a bend at the waist that indicated he had something to say. I figured this was it. This was the first step in my being invited out of that church and out of that community.

"Brother Sample," he, said "don't worry about Aunt Betsy. She's ours. We know that now. We'll take care of her." He measured out the words and said them with such determination that his language felt like a performance of what he had promised.

I thanked him. I was more grateful than he ever knew. Then as I looked over his shoulder, I could see Aunt Betsy in the church yard surrounded by four of the strongest men in the church. Each seemed to have her delicately at one of her four "corners," one under each arm and one, with work gloves on, under each knee. They were lifting her as if she were a bomb onto the back of a pickup truck. They would take her to a creek where some of the ladies of the church would "clean her up."

That night I went to see her at her "new" house. There was a pretty coal oil lamp on the table in her living room, and she sat there peaceful and calm, apparently over her earlier disturbance. She had had a good scrubbing and there was no caked dirt between her fingers or around her neck. Her dress had been washed and carefully ironed. Her self-applied makeup was only a little overdone with too much rouge and perhaps more powder than she needed, but I caught glimpses of that beautiful girl of fifty and sixty years ago. Her hair was especially dark with no crumbles of shoe polish. Someone had bought her a new can of Shinola, and the room shared its perfume.

We sat there just talking gently while I looked for the moment to say something to her. When we fell silent, I took my shot.

"Aunt Betsy, I want to say something to you, dear. I want you to know that when I'm preaching, you need to feel free to leave the church any time you want to. I won't be offended. I will know that you have a good reason."

"Oh, Brother Sample, I ain't ever gonna leave that church, no matter what."

"Aunt Betsy, I know you love me. I will never take offense if you need to go out. You can always come back."

"I do love you, Brother Sample, but it ain't you. It's those people. They love me. They really care about me. I ain't ever gonna leave that church."

And that's where we left it.

On the ride back to the college that night I tried to put together the pieces of what had transpired in Aunt Betsy's life. How did one go from being the most beautiful girl in the county married to its richest man to a "crazy" woman isolated in squalor who chased off preachers with a butcher knife? I wondered if all her collection of junk and waste at the old house was not some attempt to regain all she had lost to that thief she ran away with. And her husband—as much as he loved her, and by all accounts he adored her—placed her on such a pedestal that he incapacitated her for life without him.

What kind of ripping of reality goes on in her mind and her unconscious? I thought of cultures where one form of execution is to tie a person's legs to two crossed saplings bent to the ground and then released to split the victim limb from limb. The torque of her life seemed that wrenching. So she turns to black shoe polish to recapture the raven hair of a stolen youth and spreads smudged makeup to cover what cannot be concealed. Yet, she does not notice the buildup of dirt and soot on what was once the smooth skin of the most captivating maiden in her part of the world.

Was all of this perhaps some self-imposed punishment? Did she take herself to trial in the empty court of her own identity and then sentence herself to the incongruities of a life of beauty and ease massacred by the loss of her husband and the wiles of a seductive stranger? My point was not to establish blame. She was far too sinned against for that. But rather to grasp these fragments of a battered, torn life in some whole, to put together a flesh-and-blood puzzle. I did not want to forget the cuts around the pieces of the puzzle, but I yearned to see the fuller portrait those pieces might reveal.

Equally inexplicable, how does this little church enter into that lacerated life and embrace her after she scandalized them with her behavior and her outrageous neglect of even the most basic bodily functions? Certainly it was not my self-righteous preaching of a purloined sermon. It was not even the saintly care of Miz Anna, as dedicated and persistent as she was. Can it really be that important to have a new place in your old church: to put too much makeup on clean skin, to darken hair with new Shinola, to be placed in a clean house up and off the ground, to charge things at the store again—even cigarettes—to be welcomed to sit by people at church?

I left at the end of the summer to continue my studies at seminary. I don't know what finally happened to Aunt Betsy. She died a few years later. I doubt that she ever got over her "identity problem." So far as I know, she never again found out who she was. What did seem clear, even to her, was that she knew whose she was.

8

"IN THE GARDEN"

I never liked the hymn "In the Garden." For one thing it was too smaltzy, and I had heard it sung in such whiny and pathetic ways. I could remember how people in churches would slur from one note to the next. They moaned out the song with a kind of staged pathos. The truth of the matter is I hated the thing.

With lyrics written by C. Austin Miles, it was copyrighted in 1912 by The Rodeheaver Company who owned it. Of course, there it was, virtually unavoidable, in the *Cokesbury Worship Hymnal* used in many Methodist churches. I think I grew up singing that song at least two or three times a month.

So one day in class I decided I would "deconstruct" it. By then I was teaching at the Saint Paul School of Theology in Kansas City, Missouri, and figured I could use my authority as a seminary professor to deal it a death blow. I began by attacking its individualism. I observed to the class how often the words *I* and *me* appear: "'*I* come to the garden alone.' And it is *I* who hear the voice of God calling, 'falling on *my* ear.' And then in the chorus

Jesus walks with *me*, talks with *me*, 'And He tells me *I* am His own; And the joy *we* share'—Notice," I said, "this is a song about 'me and Jesus.'"

"But it gets worse," I claimed. "He says next in the chorus, 'And the joy we share as we tarry there, *None other has ever known.*' Can you believe," I pleaded, "the arrogance in the chorus? Does Austin Miles actually believe that no one else has ever had that kind of joy except him and Jesus? What kind of self-elevation is required to believe one's own individual experience with Jesus stands so singularly alone in two thousand years of church history?" I concluded this portion of my "critique" by asking, "Where is Christian community in this song? Where is the church? The individualism of this song is a direct assault on the Christian faith. Christian existence is *we* existence, not *me* existence," I shouted.

Then I turned to the very subjective character of the lyrics. "Notice," I observed, "how the song focuses so exclusively on the internal experience of the lyricist. He hears the voice of Jesus. He hears a melody. It is his heart that is ringing. He hears that he belongs to Jesus, and apparently hears that directly from the Lord himself."

I countered: "Jesus is more than a good feeling between your liver and your gall bladder." And picking up steam, I tried to nail it, "The Christian faith is not about sitting around staring at your navel and masturbating your feelings."

Then I made my third move. "What this song does is to move the Christian faith to the periphery of life, to a garden. That's all we need with a church already too accommodated to the culture around it: to retreat into a garden to be with this sappy idea of a Jesus who's on retreat just with me. The world is going to hell in a handbasket, and we have Christians moaning these songs about me and Jesus in a garden with birds singing, with Jesus handing out melodies and providing experiences no one else has ever known."

I also would have to say that I conveniently did not address the third verse where it says that Jesus does call us from the garden to a world of woe, but that ain't enough, I believed.

I went on: "This song was written in the first part of the twentieth century. It is one of those 'good ole songs' but it is neither good nor old. Banish it from your ministry and your worship services," I said with no little imperial finality.

The bell rang. Class was over.

I felt enormous satisfaction. I thought I had figuratively "plowed the ground" of that song and salted it. Surely nothing would grow there again.

The students filed out with those agreeing with me winking and chuckling about my "critique" and my passion. One student waited, a forty- year- old woman who came to seminary in midlife. When everyone had left, she stood before me sternly and began, "Tex, my father started screwing me when I was eleven years old. He screwed me until I was 16 when I finally found a way to stop it. After every one of those horrible ordeals I would go outside by myself and sing that song. 'I go to the garden alone while the dew is still on the roses . . . and he walks with me and talks with me and tells me I am his own.' If it had not been for that song and for Jesus walking with *me*, I would never have made it through that absolutely awful time."

My eyes dropped to the floor. I was reeling from the impact of what she had said. When I looked up, the index finger of her right hand was about two inches from my nose. It looked like a sword. In measured words she gave me an order: "Don't you ever, ever, ever make fun of that song in my presence again." With that she walked out the door.

I have never made fun of that song again except to tell her story. You see, that song for me was words on a page that I could analyze and dissect from any number of perspectives. Furthermore, I came at it from what seemed like a prison sentence of hearing it sung in the ways I had attacked in my lecture. The song had been a boring labor of moans in worship services I had known. It was not a dead formalism, but an actively vexing irritant. I did hate its individualism, its subjective character, and what I regarded as its smaltzy bathos.

But for her, the song was about a young girl isolated by her father's sexual abuse. For her that song was about survival, coping, and belonging to Jesus. She experienced the kind of criminal assault I had never known in my entire life. I learned then and there that there is not one objective way to hear or interpret a song.

More than that, her confrontation has a shining quality about it in my memory. I do not ever remember so thoroughly believing one thing and then having it so radically and definitively challenged.

Don't misunderstand; I still have problems with the hymn. When read from the perspective I read it that day, I would say most of the same things, just more gently, unless I knew the hearers well. I still don't like it. But when I am in a worship service and it is sung, I sing it with her in mind.

9

LITTLE GIRLS AND
INDIAN DOLLS

A former student of mine, Gene Barne, had invited me to preach for him at his church in northern Lee's Summit on the east side of the Greater Kansas City metro area. Before the service began, there was a time of informal moments when the congregation would share announcements or celebrations and concerns they had.

It so happened that week that the museum in Kansas City had had an exhibit called Sacred Circles, which featured Native American art and craft. At the exhibit there was also an offering for small children in which they could do arts and crafts under the direction of Native Americans who were part of the program. One little girl at the church had been part of that, and came down the aisle to the front to share her artwork from the event.

Six years old, she was terribly shy, but she was also so very proud of what she had done. Showing us the Indian doll, she was a mixture of timidity and pride, good healthy pride. In that moment she just shone. The doll was built on a two-inch square piece of cardboard. Standing up on this base was another piece of cardboard that made up the body of the doll. It was wrapped in a piece of paper, but it looked like cloth or perhaps leather. It could have represented either a blanket or a rawhide outfit of some kind. Around the waist of the doll was a bright yellow three-strand cord that was the belt. It simply tied on the front. Also on the front was a big button, a pink button, a bit too low on the doll, but nevertheless there. A cork formed the head of the doll, and the little girl had drawn a smiling red mouth consisting of a single line that turned up on each end. A small circle served as the nose, and she had drawn two eyes with one having a discernible brow. On top of the cork head was a feather, a white feather a full two inches long that dominated the head of the doll and covered no little of the meticulous face she had drawn.

It was a very nice doll, but it could not compare with the beauty of this child. As she displayed it to us, her shoulders scrunched in embarrassment, and her smile tightened into a seam across her face broken only by muffled words about the doll and how she made it. She crossed her feet back and forth, never seeming to be comfortable in a body so pulled between pride of accomplishment and nervousness before the congregation. I have seldom seen such conflicting emotions so delightfully juxtaposed. It lasted perhaps a minute, maybe two, and she returned to her parents about halfway back in the pews.

My text for the morning was from that great passage in Romans 3:21-26 where it says that all "are now justified by [God's] grace as a gift." So I worked on that idea that we are justified by God's grace as a gift that we cannot earn but rather that we can only receive as a gift. I went for about twenty minutes, and it was OK. Not great, but OK.

Just before the final hymn Gene announced that I would remain down front and invited those who wanted to visit with me to come there. After the benediction about twenty people or so came down. I noticed the little girl at the back of the line. Every time someone joined behind her, she got out of line and went to the very back. This continued until she was the last person.

When she greeted me, she handed me the Indian doll to examine.

"Oh, Honey, this is such a fine doll, but I must say I have never seen anyone more beautiful than you were this morning when you shared it with us just before the service. You just glowed," I said genuinely and handed the doll back to her. But she then handed it back to me. I guessed that she wanted to hear more. So I continued, "It really is a nice doll. It has a good base so that makes it stand up real good."

She nodded in agreement.

"And it's wrapped in a piece of paper that looks like a blanket or maybe a kind of leather outfit." I didn't say rawhide for fear she might not know what that was.

Again, she nodded, laced her fingers together, twisted her shoulders to the side, and put one finger to her lips in a guileless gesture of humility and delight. I was captivated.

"And look here, you have a yellow belt and a big pink button on the outfit. How did you ever think of that?" I continued comment to her even greater embarrassment and clear elation.

"And you drew a mouth, a nose, and eyes with eyebrows on the head."

She just beamed.

"But you know what I really like. I like the feather."

She moved her head up and down in a more energetic way to indicate that she did too.

With that I handed it back to her, but she refused it. Instead she pointed at me.

"Well, it certainly is a nice doll," I said, having run out of speeches. I then tried to give it to her again, but she pushed it back and pointed once more at me. She stopped me. I certainly didn't want to be unkind or inattentive to this lovely child, but I did not know what to say next. Then it hit me.

"Oh, Dear, you are not giving me the doll?" I said in utter disbelief.

She nodded yes in a gesture that involved her entire being.

"Oh, Dear, that is so very nice of you, but I cannot take it. It is just too much of a gift," I said, humbled by this disarmingly genuine, beautifully generous child.

Without hesitation, so help me God, she said, "That ain't what you preached!"

So as I type away on this computer, right in front of me is an Indian doll. It has a two-inch square piece of cardboard that makes it stand up straight and tall. It has a piece of paper wrapped around it that looks like a blanket or a rawhide outfit. There is a wonderful three-strand-yellow belt, and the outfit has a pink button, a large pink button, slightly low on the outfit, but nevertheless just right. The head is a cork, with a face made of a red mouth, circled nose, and two eyes, one with a big dark eyebrow. But most of all I love the feather falling rakishly across a carefully drawn face.

10

TO LOVE ONE WOMAN

My junior year the Millsaps College Band had its spring practice sessions for three days at Allison's Wells, a retreat center. My good friend, Peggy Sanford, had joined the band as a percussionist, simply because she liked the people and wanted to make the trips. I was the second-chair overly exuberant trumpet player, always too loud. So we were both there.

During a break from band practice I went swimming and was standing in about five feet of water when Peggy walked from the women's dressing room down one side of the pool. We had been friends for almost two years, but this was the first time I had seen her in a bathing suit. Her father, it seems, had told her to go and buy a new one, and to buy a good one. She spent twenty-five dollars, which at that time meant she bought the nicest bathing suit you could find in Jackson, Mississippi. It was tight around the hips and had a top in good taste, to be sure, but I saw *her* for the first time not only as a friend but also as a very desirable, sexual woman.

You see, her mother made most of her dresses, and while Mrs. Sanford was an excellent seamstress, she seemed determined to hide Peggy's body. She made these big bows that went across her chest, and then from the waist down there was a full skirt. I had no idea what she looked like in terms of her own bodily form. So far as I could tell, she was an expanse of cloth from neck to knee, except for a belt around her waist.

The bathing suit changed all of that. Before that moment I had known the love of friendship, and I had also experienced erotic, adolescent crushes. But I had never had them both at the same time for the same person. My relationships with girls and young women up until that time had been maddening, short-lived crushes. In these infatuations I never knew the girl or young woman very well. The relationships had no basis other than a temporary captivation. So after the whims of the crush ended, there was nothing to go on.

As friends Peggy and I had already shared our hopes and dreams and disclosed our failures and disappointments. We told each other the stories of our lives. I knew her family and friends. We were both deeply devoted to the church; and our commitment to the Christian faith, while certainly under major transformation as college students, undergirded our relationship in ways we hardly understood.

So when erotic passion came into our friendship, it was not mere lust or some physical longing. Rather, it ignited the previous connections in the relationship. Love for Peggy took on a different energy, not replacing the friendship, but rather permeating the affection. The erotic had content and a history. The friend-ship now had combustion.

I think of building a campfire. You can build a quick flame, for example, with a lot of pine straw. It will flash and give an immediate blaze. But a fire built slowly with good logs burns long and hot. The love and affection of friendship infused with erotic desire are not merely an itch that needs to be scratched; it is a yearning to belong, to embrace an other in a full congress of two lives, of two histories, of two bodies. It is heat, but it is torrid affection. It is physically wrenching, sensual, sexual passion, but it is the meeting of two souls who don't have to hide behind the calculated staging of a self for social consumption.

But I get ahead of myself.

I heard her sing before I ever saw her. It happened soon after I transferred to Millsaps College. Having joined the Millsaps Singers, a group of some 250 voices that sang at assemblies and chapel services, I was down on the first row with the bass section. The director, Pop King, asked a soprano to do the solo in a musical arrangement called "Lullaby on Christmas Eve" by F. Melius Christiansen.

My cousin, Bobby Day Sartin, was sitting by me and whispered, "Muscles, I want you to listen to this woman. When she sings, sugar just drips off every note. And she is just as sweet inside as she is outside. I call her 'Angel.'"

Bobby had jokingly nicknamed me "Muscles" because my lanky frame lacked sinew. Still, I did pay attention to his comment about the soprano. He wasn't kidding when he called her "Angel."

The musical piece began with the full chorus singing "Mary her vigil is keeping. . . ." Then, high above the staff, the soprano voice imitated Christmas bells: "Kling Klong, Kling Klong, Hush little babe of mine." She sang without strain, and the clarity and purity of her voice sounded like an angel. I fell in love with that voice that very afternoon.

That evening at the dining hall Bobby Day introduced me to Peggy Sanford, the soprano. "Muscles, meet 'Angel.'" She blushed at the nickname, but extended her hand. Since we were in line together, we sat down at the same table. Impressed by her talent and anxious in her presence, I began to talk compulsively.

"I'm a baseball pitcher," I offered. "Yeah, I've got a great arm. When I was a boy, my daddy would send me out with six rocks, and I would bring back six squirrels for supper. I never will forget that one day I came home with only five squirrels and my daddy just about beat me to death."

She laughed, not just a polite laugh, but a real laugh! With that I was on a roll. I ripped off a whole series of jokes, all of them about that bad; but she kept laughing, and I kept talking. She later confessed that she got indigestion from laughing so hard at my stories.

As I told her one joke after another, I watched her like a hawk, trying to foresee any boredom or tiring of my tirades or any sign that I needed to stop. When we finished supper, I walked her back to the dorm. That day, it seemed, we became fast friends, not sweethearts but friends. In the days and weeks that followed, we talked by the hour. Often we had lunch or supper together, and I walked her back to the dorm.

I remember her mouth. Not just those bright teeth, but the turn of the lips and the smile that made the corners of her mouth a delicate display of self-expression, generosity, and clarity. There simply was no surliness, no snide laughter suggesting some mocking superiority. I had heard her sing and knew how that mouth made music. A coloratura, she played with the notes around high C with a glistening timbre. More than that, her mouth said something about her character and her spirit. She seemed guileless. The way she gave herself in song seemed to be the way she became transparent to others.

After the band retreat we began to date, and as these outings mounted up, I wanted like crazy to kiss her. But I was afraid that our relationship was still one of friendship. Again, while I wanted more, I did not want to lose what we had. Nevertheless, one night I decided that I was going to kiss her, come hell or high water. We went to a movie, and afterwards I parked in the college parking lot about a hundred yards from the women's dormitory.

As we walked to the front door of the dorm, I was quiet; Peggy said later that I was unusually shy and distant. Meanwhile, I was calling myself names having to do with my cowardice and making threats about what I would do to myself if I did not have the guts to kiss her: "If you don't kiss her tonight, you will never call her or go out with her again." Or, "If you don't kiss her, you are going back to the dorm and tell them what a chicken you are." My head was a turbulence of self-extortion.

At the door we turned to say good night, and I did three things. First, I leaned forward and kissed her on the mouth. Then

I was so horrified about what she would do next, and at least as terrified about what I should say next, that I just spun on my heel and took off running. I sprinted the entire distance to the parking lot, jumped into the car, and sped away as if I had robbed a bank. All the while Peggy watched from the dorm doorstep wondering what in the world had just transpired.

Back at my room I felt like a man who had just had an illicit sexual relationship with a woman I had taken advantage of. When I got up my nerve, I called her and asked if she was OK. I worried that she felt put upon or that I had intruded on our friendship. She said she was fine, just a little concerned about me. From that time on we began to see each other much more often, and the kissing increased to my delight; but it was clear that I cared about her in ways she did not care about me.

That summer she planned to go to Chicago to study voice at the American Conservatory. I would go home to work in the oil field, my summer job that paid my way through college. The night before she left I asked if I could write her while she was gone. She said yes, and so I did, eighty-nine letters in ninety days. She later said she fell in love with me through my writing.

In August of that summer I hitched a ride on a private airplane to Chicago. Getting permission first from Peggy's mother, her voice teacher's parents let me sleep on a cot on the back porch of their apartment. But we were hardly there. For three days we left each morning at seven and went all over Chicago, coming in to sleep briefly and then off again. We were together constantly, more than we had ever been. Except for the four hours we slept each night, we were side by side taking in the Field Museums, a White Sox baseball game, an amusement park, and sightseeing on public transportation. On the last night, a beautiful evening, we went to the shore of Lake Michigan and walked and talked and had a serious conversation about what our relationship would be once we got back to Millsaps. We decided that each of us would continue to date other people, but that we would save Friday night for each other. Then, if our relationship continued to develop in its present direction, we would get engaged at Christmas and marry at the end of our senior year.

Back at Millsaps College that fall we became vitally serious about sex. We were both virgins, so we read every one of the sex manuals at the college library, six I think there were. We got all that stuff right!—at least in our heads. That May we were married and took off on our honeymoon. Yogi Berra was once asked what he thought about when he hit a baseball. Yogi dropped thoughtfully into that slump-shouldered batting stance of his, swung an imaginary bat, reflected for a moment, and said, "You can't think and hit at the same time." Well, that was our honeymoon.

We knew all we were supposed to do, but we had no skills. I don't mean we did not love each other. I don't mean we did not enjoy being together and exploring each other in all the intimate ways marriage provides. We just did not know what to do for each other. Sex had had such a big buildup that there was no way it would work for us at the outset. I could tell she was disappointed, and so was I. Our struggles continued for months after we returned from the honeymoon.

I often wonder about what would have happened had we slept together before marriage. The disappointment would have been awful given the circumstances under which such things usually occur. Our thwarted expectations would have led to a breakup. Had it done so, we would have missed the extraordinary marriage and sexual love we later found. In time the friendship and affection—and the plain fact that we just liked each other—came together with a lasting erotically filled life together.

One important ingredient of our erotic lives and our friendship was the practice of kissing. Peggy had come from a family that, while affectionate, did not do a lot of kissing. She wanted more of that kind of physical expression. I came out of a family that kissed all the time. Not only my mother, but my aunts and some of my uncles were big kissers. And my dad smacked me right on the chops from the time I can remember until he died at ninety-six years of age. So I thought kissing was just something you did, and besides, I liked it.

So, after my disastrous kiss-and-run moment at the women's dorm, Peggy and I became serious kissers. It became a practice of everyday life. Now we kiss twenty or thirty times a day. We kiss before we leave home and when we come back. We've kissed at the best times of our lives and at the worst. Just before she turned fifty years of age, she told me, "Big boy"—when she calls me "Big Boy" things are about to get significant—"if you throw a surprise party for me and call attention to the fact that I am fifty years old, you have had it!" So we flew to Denver, rented a car, and drove to the top of Rollins Pass near Winter Park. I shall never forget standing at 10,500 feet with the wind blowing and cumulus clouds making brush strokes on a blue sky. We simply stood there in all that grandeur kissing each other.

When our son was killed on his motorcycle, I was away on a speaking engagement trying desperately to get home. Though he was in a coma for twelve hours, I arrived two hours after his death. The wonderful staff at Liberty Hospital took away all the tubes, bathed Steve, and pulled him up in the bed very nearly in a sitting position. When I arrived, Peggy and I went in, sat down on the bed, and kissed him and kissed each other.

Of course, not every one shares this high view of kissing. I see these signs often in kitchens: "Kissing don't last, cooking do." I'll be hanged if that is true. I want those signs down. I can always eat out! Some say you can kiss out, too. But if you kiss out, you are going to kiss off!

My use of kissing is, in part, a metaphor here. It stands proxy for a host of practices of intimacy: touching each other as you walk by, a look of affection especially in a trying moment, making the bed together, washing dishes, vacuuming the house, caregiving when one of you is sick, or sharing with a glance a personal response when at a party or in another public setting. All these and a thousand more constitute practices of intimacy that form us and make us one.

These are acts of breathing together, of facing into the day as a unit, of one carrying the other when things don't turn out right.

It is saying "yes" to life. It is the refusal of futility and of cynicism. These practices of intimacy are the behaviors of hope, the acts of affirmation, the disclosure of the ligaments of commitment, and the muscle of conviction. Practices like these cannot be reduced to subjective feeling or "values" or ideas or psychological techniques. Life at its base is action. Life together is no different.

Yet, I don't want to get away from the physical, material practice of kissing itself. We are our bodies and, at least in our culture, the intimacy of the mouth, the taste, touch, smell, and feel of lips, teeth and tongue must represent one of the most important places of meeting and expression. To share breath in a kiss, to caress with your lips the mouth you have known across the embraces of years on end, to be lost in moments that take on their own kind of timelessness, to kiss out of deep sadness or tragedy and thereby claim what cannot be lost: these surely must be at the height and depth of intimacy.

Still, we must not leave it only to such times and events. While such moments are the most powerful and striking, there is also the peck, that quick meeting of closed lips that simply says things are all right down on the ground of our lived lives. Or, the smack of humor that shares something that is really funny or marks a moment of delight. The smack can mock kissing itself, giving yourselves distance from believing that a relationship or a kiss always has to be so serious, so monumental, or so transcendent. The beauty of kissing is its capacity to carry such a range of expression.

Furthermore, our experience is that when a relationship is in the midst of a struggle, it is time to increase the kissing. Peggy and I have a rule that when we have a fight, we kiss at some point in the conflict. It is our way of "saying" that this relationship is more important and more enduring than the fact that right now we disagree and argue. Some people disagree with this practice; they say you ought not do what you do not feel. I regard such views as a part of a pop psychology that has plagued us for the past forty years. It is exactly our feelings and the feelings between us that we want formed. I know of no better practice than kissing to express the gravity of a relationship when involved in an argument that will finally go away, or in managing a difference that may not go away but is a discordant key in the harmony of a larger symphony under way.

People often ask us how we as a couple made it through after the death of our son, a story I tell in the chapter "The Death of a Blue Jay." The amazing support we received was, of course, crucial; but I have often wondered what might have happened to us had we been individuals with a Lone Ranger spirituality. I distrust the notion that you can have conviction without institutionalizing it. I don't trust spirituality without community, the love of a couple without marriage, and life without organizations. Having seriously studied sociology now for many years, I have engaged the major criticisms of institutions and organizations; but I don't know anyone who is without these patterned forms of life, and, more especially, anyone who lives fully and well without them.

Peggy and I were carried by our long developed practices: kissing and the practices of intimacy, conversation, our dispositions about the way that God works in the world, and the conviction that God was suffering with us and for us. These things had been part of our lives for decades. They were the ways we lived. We did not have to search for them as some kind of psychological technique. They were who we were.

Perhaps this is why we did not get into the blame game, where each of us accused the other of some failure that led alchemically to Steve's death. I simply don't remember any reproach of the other. The problems we did have were those of trying too hard to take care of the other. Peggy would ask me six times in the same thirty minutes if I wanted a cup of coffee. I would ask her that same metaphorical six times if there was something she needed me to do. The exasperation with each other over these excesses of attention often broke down into laughter and then tears.

By then we had shared a lot of history. Buying a house, developing talents and skills, taking trips, nursing each other in illness, watching age come on, going through devastating losses of parents, friends, and then a son, learning that cellulite can be endearing, and that humor heals: these wedded us.

In life together we found ourselves participating in the greater reality of God. Week after week we worshiped, we prayed, and we attended to the reading of Scripture. Steve's loss not only gave gravity to issues of life and death but also sharpened our sensibilities. The spangling of stars across a luminous night, the life-giving character of a single touch, the sun filtering itself through trees to play with the ground, the capacity of a kiss to bear emotion and embody compassion, moonlight touching only the ripples of water and leaving the rest to mystery, housework that ritualized hope: these things and so many more placed us in a world embraced by God. Steve was dead, but he was not lost to God.

The party lasted past midnight. After driving home in sub-zero weather, I buried under bone-warming cover and fell into a deep Nirvana-like sleep. In a sleep without dreams gone are thoughts, aches, pains, memory, obligations, stress, and appetites. You yearn for such sleep in your worn and exhausted hours. Suddenly, the covers from Peggy's side were thrown back. She ran to the bathroom, and began making these egregious sounds. She was tossing her dinner in the onset of stomach flu.

But I wanted to sleep. I tried first not to hear her, which did not work. Then, I remembered a poster from the sixties with a quote from the psychologist, Fritz Perls, which stated: "I'm not in this world to live up to your expectations and you're not in this world to live up to mine, but if we find each other, it's beautiful." So I laid there comforting myself with this Perlian bromide. Any authority will do in a siege of self-justification.

But the irruptions from the bathroom would not cease. What's more, we had a rule: If you throw up, my job is to wring out a washrag and hand it to you, meanwhile sitting beside you, giving minimal vocal comfort and just enough of a pat not to exacerbate the malaise. The rule of course is reciprocal.

I stayed in bed, I suppose, a minute and then in a disgruntled, disrupted awakening spasm threw back the covers and shouted to myself, "Screw Fritz Perls"! In such moments, you sit there with wet washrags and futile words of comfort, and offer sleepy pats on the least engaged part of her puking body. Between heaves she apologizes for waking me up! For some strange reason I remember the day we met and her laughing at my bad jokes. Now, both of us half naked—she on her knees and me on my butt—I knew I was engaged in the school for learning intimacy. In moments like these eros becomes not sexual passion but an empathic feeling for her. Between these violent disgorgements, she reached over to hold my hand, and I realized I would rather offer her wet washrags sitting around the toilet than dance the cotillion ball with anyone else. In even wretched moments like these you find yourself participating in a Gift.

11

ERRTHY MYSTICISM

I t does not take much imagination to see the difference between that rather classical experience of mysticism I had as a college freshman and the God who "shows up" in these stories. While the stories do not, of course, represent all the ways God speaks to us, nevertheless God can be seen in broken ways in each of them. God is never captured in any experience, and certainly these few stories do not encompass the reality of God; but I hope they convey a God who shows up where we expect no such thing to happen.

An earthy mysticism reports a God who finds us in the death of a son, in moments of revelation around a toilet, in mystical judgment heavy with a wrong being done, in God's silence and absence, in confrontation that challenges us at the very point of our greatest certainties, to mention only a few. These are truly strange places for God to "appear." But God is as real in these places as in mystical experience of a more classical kind.

Further, through strange "conduits" God comes to us: in little girls with gifts that cannot be earned and in the Visions Motorcycle Club.

God comes in the love of someone who weds you in ways that defy your understanding and exceed anything you deserve. God comes in a woman who blisters your arrogance and insensitivity. God comes in the love of a congregation that surrounds a person whose squalor, drunken behavior, and outrageous acts violate their canons of respectability. And, God shows up in the music of Hank Williams, the unconditional love of a mother, and a 1940 Ford coupe.

God comes to us in Eucharist at the altar but also comes from beyond church and chancel. Eucharist comes in the life-giving "blood" of a syrup-can chalice. The very reality of that can—grit, grease, and rust—bespeaks a God who cannot be ruled out of any part of life. It is a God who sets up opposition to the walls of the world and wants them down. The body and blood of Christ come, too, in sandwiches and Kool-Aid. Such gifts, to be sure, remind us of the last supper before Christ's death, but they also enact here and now that everlasting supper where, indeed, in God we shall overcome.

Further, God's absence is a strange form of presence, and God's silence a sonic void full of sound. I certainly believe that God can "distance" God's self from us. But God's absence can also be a more powerful form of presence. That absence "resides" in the gulf between God and ourselves, as God awaits some new response from us to the opportunity of a renewed sensibility.

In these times God's silence "roars" with a sonicity beyond sound. It is the tacit Word addressed to us where blare and boom are too little. It is the hush in the presence of the unspeakable, the awe-struck before the ineffable. It is the resonant, multisensory character of Silence. It is sensibility aflame with a sensory Void.